Where Once There Were Thorns

Jeanne Wilhite Dunn

DEDICATION

This book is dedicated to the memory of my beloved mother,
Joan Helene Wechner Wilhite, who, despite our differences, always
made me feel unconditionally loved.

*****

Cover photo: Joan Wilhite
with 9 month old daughter, Jeanne in 1951

ACKNOWLEDGMENTS

This book would not have been possible without the love and support of my lifelong best friend and husband, Michael. Thank you my love! Thank you to my beloved children, Eric and Rebecca, for extending me grace while I continue to learn to be a Godly parent.
I also want to thank the dear friends who cheered me on and encouraged me through the years, including Margaret, Glenn, Janice, Pam, Kerry, Bill, and Mike S.
Special gratitude to my 'first-readers' and editors, Jeanne, Beth and Joanne for their willingness and wisdom.

Love is patient, love is kind. It does not envy, it does not boast, it is not proud. It is not rude, it is not self-seeking, it is not easily angered, it keeps no record of wrongs. Love does not delight in evil, but rejoices with truth. It always protects, always trusts, always hopes, always perseveres. Love never fails.
Corinthians 13:4-8

Chapter 1

2014

Michael and I admire the old maple trees in our front yard, as we look up at the high bare branches. We had lovingly planted these two, as little saplings over 40 years ago. Now it took the two of us, holding hands, to encircle each trunk with our arms. It is October and the maples have unleashed their burnished foliage all over the front lawn. The trees are as solid and grounded as the house that sits on our homestead. The only work they cause us in their old age, is the annual raking of the leaves. Our shoulders will be sore tomorrow, but today we laugh and chat as we rustle in the autumn leaves. The sound of crackling leaves brings to mind another October long, long ago, one that would change the course of my life forever.

*****

1967

I shuffled along through October's colorful sidewalks, ankle-deep in crackling leaves. At this time of year, naked trees lined Canastota's streets, their colorful fall garments shredded by chilly winds and scattered on the sidewalks below. Just as I stepped off the curb to cross Canal Street, a car, rumbling with a noisy engine, stopped in my path, blocking my passage to the other side of the street. The driver leaned over the front seat and rolled the passenger window down, "Want a ride home?" I recognized Michael, a classmate who I had seen just minutes before at our high school chorus rehearsal. I glanced at his deep-set brown eyes and noted his perfect eyebrows. His thick hair was the color of bittersweet chocolate and was Brylcreemed into a slicked back hairstyle just like Elvis Presley. A Pompadour, they called it. Ricky Nelson and James Dean cut and styled their hair the same way. He beamed a friendly smile my way. "Want a ride home?" he asked again.

"No thanks." I mumbled stiffly.

"Oh come on, get in," he coaxed. He leaned toward me and flipped down the inside handle of the passenger door. As the door swung open, the strains of "Happy Together" drifted out and encircled me, pulling me in as the Turtles sang something about loving somebody the rest of their life. I slid in, trying to keep my heavy load of books in front of me like a shield of armor.

I stared straight ahead at the dashboard of the black 1954 Chevy. Out of the corner of my eye, I watched as Michael shifted the car into gear. He pulled the shifting lever on the steering column back and down by reaching out with his fingers and keeping his thumb on the big, flat steering wheel. The needle on the round speedometer moved and the car began to roll. I tried to look interested in the chrome grill that covered the dash and glove box in front of me. What was I doing in a car with a boy that I hardly knew? I thought about how this kid acted up in chorus rehearsals and was often reprimanded by the director. I would have been so humiliated if I had been singled out, but it never seemed to bother Michael.

We first became aware of each other in chorus, an extracurricular activity available at Canastota High

School. The chorus was practicing for a musical production, *South Pacific*, and Michael and his best friend, Harry, were cast as sailors. I was singing in the backup chorus while Michael and Harry danced around the stage showing off for the girls.

I learned from friends that he had his own car, always wore a denim jacket, and smoked cigarettes. That, in my book, made him what we called a 'hood.' There were several hoods in our school and these boys were the rebels, the ones who drove fast cars, were not particularly interested in studying and who tested the boundaries at school and in the community.

Michael was definitely not my type, nor was I his. High on his priority list was tinkering with the engine on his 14-year-old car in Juggy's garage. Juggy, the school grease monkey, was a classmate who invited kids to work on their hotrods in his dad's garage. Mike's second priority was his weekend job at a well-drilling company. He also enjoyed showing off by walking around the high school stage on his hands. I, on the other hand, was a shy animal-lover and placed great importance on my schoolwork and being accepted by my small circle of friends.

Michael drove to the other side of town where I lived. It occurred to me that he might take me on a wild ride, complete with squealing tires and fast speeds. I had seen him pull out of the student parking lot, spewing gravel and squealing the tires as they connected with the pavement on Roberts Street. But he was considerate of me, or maybe it was the quiet neighborhood in which I lived. Without fanfare, he drove right into our driveway.

"Nice house," he said.

"Yea, my mom and dad built it themselves when I was a baby."

"Cool."

He turned the key in the ignition and the rumbling motor and music hushed. My beloved Boxer, Chipper, charged across the lawn and bounced around the car. My dog was my first love, but today I ignored his antics. I watched as Mike pushed in the cigarette lighter below the steering wheel and turned to face me.

"Thanks a lot," I said, just barely able to get my dry mouth to work.

I moved to open the door and Michael said, "Wait a minute. Would you like to go out with me this Saturday night?"

He lit a cigarette as if he had done it hundreds of times before and stared at me. I felt myself turning as red and hot as the round heating element on the end of the cigarette lighter. He blew a plume of smoke out the driver's side window and looked at me intently. Although the radio was no longer playing, my heart pounded the reverberations of "Happy Together" in double time. I was sure Mike could hear it.

"No, I can't. I have to babysit." I finally squeaked out. Panicked and breathless in the awkward moment, I made a hasty decision. I fumbled through my things, drew out a calendar planner book, and said, "See, right there, I have to babysit Saturday night." Secretly, deep down I wanted to flirt with disaster, take a chance, go on a date, and get to know this boy in the denim jacket with his collar turned up. Nevertheless, I chose to seal my fate with this concrete evidence, an entry in my calendar book.

Michael gently tugged the little planner from my hands and pointed to a weekend that was blank.

"How about this Friday night? You don't have to babysit this night." I tugged my knee socks up and pulled my skirt down over my bare knees. I smiled, feeling somehow rescued and relieved that this boy had completely turned the situation around in such a matter-of-fact way. Suddenly I felt like I was someone of worth!

For the first time since I had climbed into his car, empowered, I looked Michael right in the eye and said, "OK then. It's a date."

"I'll pick you up at seven," he said, and I slipped out of the car. I scampered up the steps to the front door, too shy and embarrassed to hang around his car or say anything more. Chipper bounced and snorted around me at the door, his stubby tail a vibrating comma.

I went inside and immediately peeked out the living room window to watch Michael back out of the driveway and disappear down the street. I turned and my mother was watching me intently.

"Who was that?" she asked, and she peered out the same curtained window.

"His name is Mike Dunn and he sings in chorus with me," I replied, trying to make it sound like we were more friends than just acquaintances. "He asked me out." I held my breath and my Mom said nothing, but made a little sound of disgust, pulling her tongue from the roof of her mouth.

I followed her into the kitchen where the smell of Hungarian goulash filled the air. Jamie, my 3-year-old brother, was busy smearing wet graham crackers all over the Formica kitchen table. Mom sat down, shook a Salem cigarette out of the familiar aqua blue pack and lit it. She crossed her thin legs and began moving her right foot in little circular motions as it dangled there in mid-air. I noted this and tried to vacate the room and avoid the mounting tension.

"Jeanne," she said, and I took a deep breath and stopped in my tracks. I turned and watched her familiar fidgeting, fingering a book of matches. "You don't need to be going out with any boys. Who is that boy anyway?" she spat out as though I had deceived her and woven a web of lies about him. She was so hard to understand. She often had hidden meanings in what she actually verbalized and double messages were standard.

"Mom, he's a senior like me and he sings in chorus. He plays one of the sailors in *South Pacific*. He seems like a nice guy." The baby, Mikey, began to whimper in his crib, awake now from his afternoon nap. Mom snuffed out her cigarette disgustedly and rose to get the baby. I took the opportunity to escape to my room upstairs with a glass of Grape Kool-Aid.

I flopped on my bed and stuck my thumb in my mouth. My shameful little secret, I thought to myself with disgust. I grabbed the hem of the pillowcase and began rubbing it on my nose and upper lip. I had sucked my thumb for as long as I could remember. No attempts to stop during childhood had met with success. My parents had tried putting rubbing alcohol on my thumb at 5, threatened that I would have bucked teeth at 10 and embarrassed me at 13 by telling family friends that I still sucked my thumb. The plain truth was that at the age of 17 I still shoved my thumb into my mouth when I was alone. I lied when family asked if I had finally stopped and I was successful in keeping it a secret. I hated myself.

Now that my older sister, Lynn, was gone, it was easier to keep my secret. Lynn, four years older than me, was a flight attendant and lived in Utica. With her room vacated, I had the entire upstairs to myself. I could suck my thumb whenever I wanted or until I heard footsteps on the stairs.

When I was 7 years old, an undiagnosed appendicitis led from a ruptured appendix to peritonitis and a long hospital stay. I was critically ill and spent the better part of a month in the Lenox Memorial Hospital on the corner of Center and Main Street in Canastota. I was very sick and had endured pain, fear, and many unpleasant treatments. I learned early on that sucking my thumb was a way I could control my feelings of vulnerability. I used that as my excuse in my own mind. Now, at 17, I no longer felt the need to actually suck on my thumb, but it still comforted me to feel it resting on my tongue. I created a variety of ways to fold the fabric of hems so I could rub them on my nose and lip while my thumb was in my mouth. I didn't know my humiliating habit would become a lingering, shameful secret.

I turned on my radio and changed into jeans and a sweater. As I settled in to do my homework, I listened as the news reporter spoke of thousands of Vietnam war protesters gathering in Washington for a peaceful rally at the Lincoln Memorial. I sipped my Kool-aid pensively. A peaceful protest was unheard of in this household.

A happy heart makes the face cheerful,
but heartache crushes the spirit.
Proverbs 15:13

Chapter 2

Tonight is date night for Michael and me. We have set aside Tuesday evenings for the past two decades as our night out. We are careful to protect this time. We are going out to dinner, our usual Tuesday night activity. It is easy, with our lives so full and busy, to drift apart. I teach puppy obedience classes on Wednesday nights and Mike does his civic duty by serving on the Town of Lenox Zoning Board of Appeals on Thursday evenings. I take watercolor painting classes on Thursday evenings and meet with fellow writers on Monday nights. Mike has church board meetings and youth group activities. And those are just the evening activities, so it's important that we keep this weekly commitment to renew our bond and focus on each other. It seems so long ago, but I remember in vivid detail my first date with Michael.

*****

The Friday night Michael had pointed out in my calendar book arrived. I changed my sweater four times before deciding on the burgundy one with pink snowflakes around the neckline. Maybe he'll take me to the movies tonight. *The Graduate* was playing at the Oneida Kallet Theater. I had only had one date before this date with Michael and I really didn't know what to expect. Would he take me for something to eat? Bowling? Roller skating? All I knew was that Mike would pick me up at seven and we were double dating with my best friend, Cathy and her date, Jim. It didn't occur to me to ask what we would be doing on this date. Cathy and I had talked endlessly about the upcoming date and she knew as little about Jim as I did Michael.

When Michael pulled into the driveway, I yanked the front door open, yelled, "Bye!" to my parents and flew out the door. I didn't wait to see if Michael would come to the door to pick me up and meet my parents.

I was not popular with the boys in my school by any stretch of the imagination. I was never asked out on dates or to parties. The only boy who took an interest in me was from another town and did so two weeks before he was drafted into the Navy. We went to the movies once before he left for boot camp and he kissed me once politely by the front door. The relationship became a letter-writing marathon for several months and then just fizzled out. That was the extent of my experience with boys. When Cathy and I talked about boys, it was always regarding which of our friends were dating which boys. Neither Cathy nor I had boys interested in us. It hurt that I wasn't sought after like so many of my friends. To fill the void in my social life, I busied myself with obedience training my dog and horseback riding. When I was 13, my father bought me a pony and although the pony had long since been sold, I still had friends with horses and I loved to ride more than anything. I worked hard to get good grades in school. It was more important to me to use a study hall to get work done than it was to flirt with boys.

I tried to watch the most popular girls to determine what it was that attracted the teenage boys. I came to believe that they were much prettier than I was and looks apparently had lots to do with one's appeal. I was taller than most in my class and had unmanageable thin straight hair that fell like limp corn silk every day on the long walk to school. I tried to curl my hair in brush rollers, Spoolies or Bobby pins but the damp, early morning air ruined my carefully arranged hairdo day after day. The boys wanted the girls with hair teased into a big bubble on top and that flipped upwards on the ends. That certainly left me out. But tonight someone was interested in me! I was going on a date!

When I reached the idling car, Jim jumped out so I could get in the front seat with Michael. "Scoot over!" he smiled and he crowded into the front seat, sandwiching me between him and Mike. I felt awkward and found myself trying to shrink so there would be no bodily contact on either side. I shoved my folded hands between my thighs and pressed my legs together until my muscles began to ache with fatigue.

We arrived at Cathy's house where she and Jim got into the back seat. I was aware of how close I was to Michael while they folded the front seat forward so they could climb into the back, but as soon as they were situated, I slid over to the passenger door. I cranked opened the triangular vent window and let the cool air fill the car. "So where are we going?" I asked.

"It's a surprise," Jim said. "Want a stick of Teaberry Gum?" he asked, waving a pink paper-wrapped stick in front of my face.

"No, thank you," I murmured. We drove to the local pool hall, Mike parked the car and told Cathy and me that they would be right back. Both boys disappeared into the pool hall and returned within minutes. We asked no questions and did not get an explanation as to why we made this stop. It would be much later that I would learn our dates had gone into the pool hall to purchase condoms.

"OK, we are on our way!" announced Michael happily. The conversation was light in the car and made the time go quickly. I paid no attention to where we were headed, until Michael turned onto a dirt road that led to a cluster of lakefront cottages on Oneida Lake.

"What are we doing here?" I asked as we bumped along, suddenly troubled and afraid. "We're going down to my friend Bubby's camp," he responded. As we pulled into the driveway, the unlit cottage loomed in the darkness like an ugly squatting toad.

"No one is home," Cathy observed dubiously.

"It's OK. My buddy said we can use it."

Hopeful, I got out of the car with the others, thinking we might turn on the lights, make popcorn, and play cards or a board game. I didn't know there was no electric service to the camp. I stumbled in the dark and Michael took my hand. Feeling the warmth of his hand, I giggled and followed him inside.

"Where are we going?" I asked, tripping again. I heard Cathy and Jim somewhere else in the camp.

"Come here," Michael whispered, and as I heard the squeak of bedsprings, he pulled me down to where he sat. I slammed down on the edge of the bed and Mike began to kiss me. I felt like I was smothering and I tried to wiggle away. Michael, silent now, grabbed at my body, pushed me back on the old bed and covered me with his body.

"Don't, please don't," I gasped, as I tried to avert his groping hands. I struggled to free myself.

Like a breathless, wild animal, he panted in my ear, "Come on, will you just relax?" The sound of his voice brought me back from the edge of terror, and I began to cry. He climbed off me and I scrambled to the edge of the bed, crying in fear, anger and disappointment. Michael began cursing as I smoothed my sweater in the dark. He stomped across the floor and I watched his dark shadow as he bent to yank his shoe off. He hurled the shoe across the murky room and it narrowly missed my head and crashed into the wall.

"Son of a bitch," he rumbled. I sat motionless except for my uncontrolled sniveling, fearful I might escalate his anger even more. He's going to kill me now and no one will ever find me out here.

Finally, when Michael's tirade began to wane, I ventured, "Would you please take me home?"

"Yup," he said flatly. He fumbled in the blackness and recovered his shoe. As he sat on the edge of the squeaky bed to put his shoe on, I rose instantly and moved away. "I'm sorry, Jeanne," he said quietly. "I'll take you home." He called to Jim and Cathy and the four of us piled back into the old car. I looked at the clock on the dashboard and noted we had only been in Bubby's camp for 11 minutes. I was as exhausted as if we had spent hours trekking across a mountain range.

We drove Cathy to her house first. She and I barely exchanged words on the ride home. In fact, the car was remarkably quiet for being occupied by four 17 year olds on a Friday night. Jim asked to be dropped off again at the pool hall. He climbed out of the car and I was keenly aware that I was alone again with Michael. He turned the ignition off and turned slightly to face me.

"Jeanne, I am so sorry about what happened tonight," he began. "I just didn't know." I was silent but I looked into his eyes, confused by his remark. I was sure he was angry with me, but he continued. "I thought you were one of those fast girls," he explained. "The guys down at Juggy's garage were talking about you a few weeks ago and they told me you were fast. I never would have treated you like that, but they all said they had been out with you and you were always ready for a good time, if you know what I mean."

I nodded, knowing exactly what he meant. "You've got to be kidding!" I answered. "I don't even go out with boys, Mike! No one in school is interested in me. And I certainly haven't been out with any of the guys that hang out at Juggy's!" Michael and I both began to laugh at my remark and the tension began to dissipate.

"Well then, the joke's on me," Michael contemplated. "Wait 'til I see them." He rubbed his chin thoughtfully and seemed to be formulating a plan of some kind in his mind.

I stared at him as the streetlight in front of the pool hall illuminated the front seat of the Chevy. He had a kindness about him that I had not noticed before. He made some silly remarks that caused me to laugh. When I laughed he smiled back at me, obviously pleased. I liked his sense of humor and he seemed to enjoy making me chuckle.

"It's only a quarter to eight. Would you like to ride around for a while before I take you home?" he asked suddenly serious. "No funny stuff. I promise," he assured me. I nodded and my heart melted.

Michael started the car and began the shifting sequence I had already become familiar with. I watched everything he did, suddenly curious and delighted with his every move. He put a cigarette to his lips and I pushed the dashboard lighter in and handed it to him, smiling. I felt like we were sharing a secret ritual, even though I didn't smoke. I felt like I knew what he needed. We began to talk about school, family, birthdates, opinions, milestones in our lives. There was so much to talk about!

The car hummed through the quiet streets of our village, out to the country and back again, but neither one of us paid attention to where we were. The only world that mattered to us that evening was inside Michael's car. He seemed genuinely interested in me and asked question after question. I had never experienced this kind of attention before. When he looked directly into my eyes as he talked, I blushed inexplicably. He listened intently to everything I said. When he spoke, there were no hidden meanings in what he said.

At last, we found ourselves just outside Canastota and Michael suggested that we see if we could find his best friend, Harry. "I bet he's at Gladys's house," he said. Gladys and Harry were a long-time steady couple at our school and Mike was sure we would find them together. When we reached her house, Michael parked the car well off the left shoulder of the country road, right at the steps leading up to the front door. Sure enough, as the engine quit, Harry and Gladys appeared in the doorway. I ducked my head to watch out the drivers' window as they bounced down the front steps hand in hand. "Hey guys!" Mike called.

As they neared the car, Harry peered in and asked, "Who's that you got with you, Mike?"

I slid to the center of the seat right next to Mike as he told them, "Jeanne Wilhite. We went out tonight." He turned and winked at me. I was pleased to think we already had a secret between us.

"Hi Harry! Hi Gladys!" I called. We remained in the car and they sat on the grassy slope next to us. The four of us visited for a long time. The talk was easy and laughter bubbled up often. Occasionally I leaned comfortably on Michael as we chatted. Michael and I saw how Harry and Gladys cared for and appreciated each other. I noted how comfortable they were with one another, how easily words of affirmation were exchanged. They were a teenage couple in love, bound by Harry's class ring on Gladys's finger. It seemed that we somehow mirrored this couple, even though this was our first date. I felt it strong and wonderful as we sat there. Like a fish on a line, love was tugging on my heartstrings. I would learn later that Mike felt it too.

Mike dropped me off 15 minutes before my curfew. I never did return to the passenger side of the seat when we left our friends. I felt perfectly comfortable right beside Michael and I wanted to be sure he knew it.

I knew he felt the same when he gently reached for my hand and our fingers intertwined as if they had done so a million times before.

"Thanks for a great time." I offered simply, when we pulled into the driveway at my house. As I got out of the car, Michael smiled but did not attempt a goodnight kiss. I floated up the front steps as Mike drove away, taking my heart with him.

Jeanne Wilhite Dunn

Who of you by worrying
can add a single hour to his life?
Matthew 6:27

Chapter 3

Our daughter, Rebecca, and I are getting ready for a trip to the Midwest to do some genealogy investigative work. We thumb through a box of yellowed letters that my mother and father wrote to each other during the brief period of time that they were dating. Reading them confirms the story that my mother told Lynn and me about the day she met Dad.

*****

On May 8, 1945, the world was celebrating the end of World War II and my father, James Roscoe Wilhite, found himself in New York City for the celebration. He disembarked his Coast Guard ship, the

USS Knoxville, anchored in New York Harbor. He followed the throngs of shouting, jubilant flag wavers to Washington Square in Greenwich Village.

It was there he struck up a casual conversation with my mother, Joan Wechner. She had skipped out of boarding school that day, as she often did. She took the subway south along 5th Avenue to the bohemian hangout she loved. Joan intended to treat herself to an ice cream soda. After all, she had just celebrated her 17th birthday the day before.

As she wandered through the crowds, she spotted my father. His mahogany red, wavy hair and quiet demeanor were most attractive. They introduced themselves and found a comfortable place to sit near the Washington Square Arch. Joan, with lovely thin legs and high cheekbones bubbled on like the fountain splashing in the middle of the square. The beautiful iconic arch sheltered the couple as they chatted easily and got to know one another. They found that they had similar backgrounds. Her parents divorced when she was very young and she was placed in St. Christopher's Boarding School in Dobbs Ferry, on the Hudson River, north of the city.

Although she saw her parents on special occasions, she did not experience a traditional family life. She was an only child and my father might have well been *too, since he never knew his parents or siblings. Like two young waifs, they were drawn to each other, both desperately seeking to ease the pain of loneliness and abandonment. She was talkative, fun, always ready for a wild dare and had been the leader in all mischievous escapades at the boarding school. My father was quiet, intelligent, and meticulous in all his endeavors.*

Opposites in many ways, the two ignored their character differences and let their similar circumstances seal their fate. That summer my mother and father were together, celebrating the end of war and the beginning of their love.

*****

The Saturday morning after my first date with Michael I felt different, but I had no one to confide in, no one with whom I could share this delicious secret. I decided it was best not to discuss this new experience with my Mom, after hearing her comments on dating. After hearing the story of my parents' first meeting so many times, I was sure Mom must have felt then, the same way I did now, hopeful and almost buoyant. However, her remarks about the triviality of dating prompted me to keep the giddiness of new love to myself.

Mom and I stripped the sheets from the beds upstairs and began the laundry. I ran up and down the basement stairs to put load after load into the washing machine, hidden in the gloom of the basement. I hung the freshly laundered sheets and towels on the backyard clothesline while Mom bathed and dressed the boys. It seemed like a routine Saturday, but I felt like the world had changed somehow. I wondered if she could see the change in me. Did she know I was thinking about Michael continuously? Did she know I couldn't wait to see him again?

The kitchen smelled of freshly brewed coffee and I knew my father was there, frying eggs and bacon and burning toast, as he did every Saturday morning. When we sat down to eat breakfast, I dreaded the prospect of conversation.

"So how was the date?" my mother asked, without looking up, as she chopped a banana on Jamie's plate.

"Good," I answered, trying to sound nonchalant.

"So what did you do?" she countered, and she spooned oatmeal into Mikey's open mouth. I was aware that my heart rate had accelerated and suddenly my appetite left me. A piece of bacon momentarily lodged itself in my dry throat.

"Answer your mother," my father prodded. I knew better than to lie, but I didn't want to share all of what had happened the night before. It was too precious and personal to share when there was a chance I would be forbidden to see Mike again. Besides, they would get the wrong idea about him.

"Well, we went for a drive down by the lake and then over to Gladys Brown's house." All true, I thought to my clever self.

Of course, this response did not satisfy Mom. As she gently scraped oatmeal off Mikey's chin with the spoon, she probed, "Is that it? Doesn't sound like much of a date to me. Where do his people live anyway? Why did he ask *you* out?" I was sure I heard the emphasis on 'you,' as though I were some sort of ugly social reject. Rather than try to answer the barrage of inquiries, I shrugged my shoulders and dipped my toast into the egg yolk. Dad said nothing, nibbled his bacon, and listened intently to President Johnson on the radio.

"I have homework to do," I said, "May I be excused?"

I went upstairs and sat at the desk in my room. I looked out the window and down on to Stroud Street. Leaves turned cartwheels on the pavement and then came to rest at the curb where they piled up. Without thinking, I slipped my thumb into my mouth and rubbed the hem of my sweatshirt on my upper lip. It seemed like yesterday I was doing cartwheels and handstands on the front lawn.

What had happened to that blithe time? Why was it that every time my parents, especially my mother, said something to me, it annoyed me?

Dad was generally easy going and he and I got along well. Perhaps it was because I shared his love of the outdoors and nature. He worked for the USDA as a soil conservationist. When I was younger, I found his office downtown irresistible. Every time I visited there I hauled out the big illustrated volume of trees native to New York State. I carefully inspected the rock and mineral samples that lined the shelves and examined the maps that hung on the walls.

At home, he was quiet and let Mom, the pivotal person in our troubled family, rule pretty much everything. She used to threaten us, "You girls are going to get it when your father gets home." But we didn't. However, when my father lost his temper, he whipped off his belt and Lynn and I would feel the sting of leather on our behinds.

I felt smothered and irritated that Mom had so much control over every aspect of my life. She read my diaries, snooped in my dresser drawers, and listened in on phone calls. I resented her constant invasion of my privacy. I wanted a little independence.

I was still daydreaming when my mother turned the doorknob and entered my room. My thumb flew out of my mouth and my hand landed in my lap under the desk, knuckles scraped. "Geez, Mom, I could have been changing my clothes! Can't you ever knock?" I complained.

Ignoring my words, she sat down on my bed and felt the bare mattress cover with the back of her hand. I knew she was checking for fresh pee stains. Suddenly I was angry with her. I was 17 and still wet the bed sometimes. When I did, I used my hair dryer to dry the sheets before I left for school to avoid being caught. How ironic the situation was. I was old enough to want to fix my hair so the boys might notice me, but for some reason beyond my comprehension, I still woke up some mornings in a cold, wet bed. The hairdryer ritual left my room stifling hot and reeking of urine, so I cracked the window open before I left for school, even in the dead of winter. If my mother found out the bed was wet again, I would be in for another humiliating talk with questions I couldn't answer. I just didn't know how to stop. The mattress cover was dry this time.

"Jeanne, I don't think it's a good idea for you to be hanging around that boy. You have to be careful around boys who are your age." I was silently loathing her at that moment. I did not want any intimate woman-to-woman talks with her, not now, not ever. I wanted her to get out of my room.

"You will be going to college next year, so you need to concentrate on your schoolwork right now. You don't need to be dating any boys." I was quiet. "OK, Babe?" she concluded.

I snarled, "No!" and turned back to my unopened books.

She got up to leave, seemingly oblivious to my frustration and anger, and further aggravated me by instructing, "You'd better bundle up tomorrow. The temperature is going down into the 40's tomorrow and Monday." I rolled my eyes behind my mother's back. I knew how to dress and I was not a baby.

Children, obey your parents in the Lord, for this is right. Honor your father and mother, which is the first commandment with a promise, that it may go well with you and that you may enjoy
long life on the earth.
Ephesians 6:1-3

Chapter 4

Monday morning I dug out my green corduroy winter coat and a black and green striped scarf as I prepared for the mile walk across town to school. As I gathered my load of books, my mom called from Jamie and Mikey's room, "Wear your lightweight red jacket." The queen of double messages, she had confounded me again. I was never sure of what it was she wanted. It occurred to me for the first time that I no longer cared what she wanted. I yanked off the winter coat, threw it over her rack of jazz albums next to the stereo and stomped out the door.

I set out for school anxious to see Mike again. A block from home I spotted the black Chevy Bel-Air cruising slowly up Hickory Street toward me. Michael stopped the car and I hopped in. He turned down the blaring radio. I was pleased that Mike still seemed as enamored with me as I was with him. "So, are we going to go out again?" he asked, as I hauled the heavy door shut. I nodded happily and got a pleasantly weird sensation in my chest, like tiny birds fluttering their wings.

At school, I found Cathy. "What happened with you and Jim on Friday night?" I asked.

She slammed her locker shut and turned to me, shifting a heavy load of books, "Nothing, thank God! He's cute but what a creep he is! He tried to get fresh with me and I was so glad when Mike called us to go. I was scared to death! I can't believe they took us to that dumpy place."

"Yeah, I know," I answered. The bell rang for first period class to start. "I'll call you tonight and tell you about me and Mike," I promised and we hurried off in opposite directions.

Mike drove me home from school every day that week and by Wednesday, it was evident that my mother intended to be there in the window every day, scrutinizing our time together like a sober-faced sentry. There was no expression on her face as she watched out the window, the curtain pulled back and her face close to the pane. I had the distinct feeling that Michael would not be welcome in the house. I thought possibly it was because he drove a car that was 14 years old. She might like a boy who drove a newer car, maybe a nice Ford Fairlane. She liked nice things. Despite Mom's watchful eye, we sat in the car and talked.

"Hey," Mike said suddenly, "I saw the guys at Juggy's garage last night. I asked them which ones had been out with you and they all started to backtrack. They all admitted they had never been on a date with you at all. I told them if any one of them ever said anything more about you, they would have to answer to me." He pushed a lock of hair out of my face and smiled.

"Wow, I said, impressed, "Thanks for sticking up for me." We remained in the car in the driveway saying our goodbyes, not wanting to part. I looked up at the window. "We're being watched," I said to Michael without moving my lips. It made us both laugh nervously, but I knew there was nothing funny about what was happening.

That night I telephoned my best friend. When I told her about how Michael and I had spent the rest of the evening together, she obviously disapproved. "Are you kidding me?" she lectured, "Jeanne, he's not for you. He's a hood! He took us to an abandoned camp, for Pete's sake!"

I countered, "But he's a really nice guy. I had fun with him, Cathy. And I think he really likes me! We are so much alike!" I explained how Mike made me feel like I was important when I was with him. He seemed to understand everything I shared with him. When I added that he had apologized for his ill-mannered behavior at Bubby's camp, Cathy finally conceded.

"Whatever," she sighed, "but I can't believe you drove around with him. You are crazy for hanging out with him. I have to go. I have trig homework to do." Our phone conversation ended with disappointment on both ends of the phone line. Cathy seemed disappointed that I found Michael attractive and I felt the same way about my friend after listening to her reprimand me like an old grandmother.

After several weeks, my mother gave me an ultimatum about my growing friendship with Mike. "I told you, I don't want you going out with that kid. He is trouble," she prophesized. I wondered where she got her information and why she made such a determination. I had no intention of ending my relationship with him. Mom often made rulings that I, for the most part, ignored.

She would often prohibit something, only to allow and even embrace it the next day. So I ignored her remark.

I decided that it was time for Michael to meet my mother and father. We had been on several dates, despite my mother's notion that I should not be dating boys, and I had not asked him to come in to meet my parents. He had not offered either. I sensed that he had issues with low self-esteem and figured he felt uncomfortable about meeting them. His parents certainly did not help his self-confidence. In fact, they pretty much ignored him. "I don't think they like me," he protested, as I pulled him by the hand over the grass on the front lawn.

"We should have done this weeks ago," I chided. Both my parents were civil and reserved upon meeting Mike. They asked where he lived and about his family.

Mike cheerfully explained, "We live out in the country, not far from Oneida Lake. I guess you could say we're country bumpkins." I hoped that they liked his good-natured temperament. They were not nasty, but I could sense their disapproval. I didn't understand why. I had met Mike's family and they were very nice folks in the same socio-economic position as our family. We both knew that an early introduction was the respectful and considerate thing to do, but I put it off because I was afraid it might jeopardize our growing relationship somehow.

The fact that Michael smoked cigarettes alone, could be cause for condemnation. Both my parents smoked, but in our household, it was common that something might be OK for one person and not for another. Incongruence was the order of the day in our family.

My father quickly found common ground with Mike. They both enjoyed working on cars. Dad seemed impartial, but my mother took an obvious dislike to this new man in my life. It wasn't until years later that I began to understand that my mother was jealous and threatened by a boyfriend who might, in her eyes, rob her of my love and devotion. She was desperate to feel loved and her need to control everyone emotionally, unfortunately caused her to raise emotionally crippled children, including me.

But I knew I had found a diamond in the rough in Michael. She may have seen Mike as a threat to her closely supervised family, but to me he represented a ticket to my independence and for her, the thought of that was unimaginable. I was soon to discover that leaving the nest was going to be a monumental undertaking.

Michael called every night and after 10 minutes, my father would usually remind me that I had homework to do. One evening I ignored my father's prompting. "I've gotta go," I whispered reluctantly into the phone.

As though he hadn't heard me, Mike continued on, "Wait. Listen to this." I heard a country crooner sing a little ditty and guitar strings resonated through the phone.

"Michael," I repeated, "I heard your radio. My father says I have to hang up now."

"No, that wasn't a radio. That was me," he answered.

"Get out of here! It was not! Was that really you?" It was hard to believe that Michael was making the lovely music coming through the telephone line, but I did recognize his voice. So I discovered that my new beau was a gifted musician, as well as a talented vocalist.

"Get off the phone! Now! I'm expecting a call," Dad barked.

We said our good-byes as I untangled the knot I had wound in the telephone cord.

We continued to date all through that fall, but neither of us had much money to spend on anything. I earned 50 cents an hour for occasional babysitting, so I was no bottomless money pit. All of Mike's earnings from his well-drilling job went for insurance and gas for his car. We spent lots of time driving around Madison County. Gasoline was about 35 cents per gallon at Finn's Gas Station on Route 5, so we could enjoy hours of being together rather inexpensively. We discovered back roads that trailed over the undulating hills of our county. Driving them was like riding a roller coaster and we named them 'tummy roads' because, if we were going fast enough, the dips and rises in the roads momentarily made our stomachs experience 0 gravity.

So we were content to ride in the car, rain or shine. It became our sanctuary, a place to talk freely, and a place to be ourselves. After the disastrous first date encounter, we were careful to limit our physical contact to brief kisses and lots of handholding. Seat belts were not yet part of automobile design, so I was able to scoot over to the middle of the front seat, where I could sit beside Mike and hold his hand.

We often parked at the top of Chittenango Falls and admired the dazzling colors of autumn and the crashing waterfalls. We had so much to talk about. We drank in each others words, thirsting to learn all we could about each other.

We went to the drive-in once before it closed for the season. I had never been to such a venue before and was intrigued that once we found a good spot, there was a small berm upon which we drove the front wheels. This tilted our windshield up toward the huge outdoor screen to maximize viewing of the movie. Michael figured out how to hook the heavy metal speaker to the window of the car and we were all set. I looked around in the growing darkness and noticed, in cars on all sides of us, young pony-tailed girls and their dates. We gobbled popcorn as we watched and listened to Lulu belt out the title song of the feature film, *To Sir With Love*. Suddenly, Mike began fumbling with my fingers with determination. "What are you doing?" I asked, annoyed that he was distracting me from the movie.

"I'm trying to get you to go steady with me!" he stated, as he slid his bulky class ring over my left ring finger.

"Oh!" was all I could say, before he drew me close and kissed me. Going steady meant that we were exclusively dating each other and not interested in other people. I was thrilled that he wanted me for his own. I accepted his ring and decided I would wear it for my parents to see. When I got home, I dug out some yarn and wrapped it round and round the band until the ring fit on my finger without slipping off. My parents never said a word about it.

I found it quite disturbing that Mom, especially, was silent about it. I was prepared for some kind of conflict. Perhaps she remained silent about the ring as a way of pretending that my relationship with Michael wasn't moving to the next level. While I was growing up, conflict seemed to be normal, but as I got older and became more aware of the way other families behaved, I began to realize my mother had some serious control issues.

Jeanne Wilhite Dunn

Finally, brothers, whatever is true, whatever is noble, whatever is right, whatever is pure, whatever is lovely, whatever is admirable—if anything is excellent or praiseworthy—think about such things.
Philippians 4:8

Chapter 5

It is Christmas once again and I sit by the fire and stare at the bare Christmas tree. Michael comes in from the barn, stomping his boots at the back door. "Everybody OK and tucked in for the night?" I ask, referring to our menagerie of farm animals.

"Yes, and here's six eggs from your girls," he says as he empties his pockets of half a dozen dark brown eggs. My husband washes up and joins me to trim our

tree. My back aches often now from years of pounding fenceposts and carrying feed bags, so he volunteers to carry three big boxes of decorations downstairs from the attic.

"We have way too many things to hang on the tree. It takes forever!" I complain, not really meaning what I proclaim.

"Well Honey," Mike says, "you can pick out the ones that have to go." We both laugh, knowing that our collection of ornaments from around the world is too precious to pare down. How our Christmas celebrations have changed over the years! We have become parents and grandparents very much like those who once made our childhood holidays bright. In my heart, I can still feel the wonder and excitement my mother created when Christmas was near.

*****

My sister was home for Christmas and I chattered about my newfound love. I told her I was going steady and showed her Michael's ring. I knew my mom and dad had noticed I was wearing Michael's ring, but still they chose not to comment on it. I could tell Lynn things that I wasn't comfortable telling my mother. We discussed how to tell if one was really in love. I decided I was in love with Michael. I was sure of it.

Lynn and I went Christmas shopping at WT Grant's Department Store in Oneida. I found a beautiful navy blue Fisherman's knit sweater, with traditional cable stitching down the front. I knew Michael would look rugged and handsome in this sweater. Every time I saw him he wore the same denim jacket and I knew the sweater would be a nice change. He didn't seem to have much of a wardrobe. The sweater was $15.00. I had that much money, but if I made this purchase, I would have little left to buy gifts for my family. I bought the sweater and swore Lynn to secrecy.

At home, Lynn and I decorated the Christmas tree, while Jamie handed us the ornaments. We gave one-year-old Mikey an unbreakable angel tree-topper to play with while we worked. We reminisced about Christmases past, long before Jamie and Mikey were born and how fun it had been when we were kids. Years ago, grandparents came to visit or we drove to Long Island to spend the holidays with Mom's family. Even though she had no siblings, she had aunts and uncles. Her parents were divorced and had both remarried.

We had an odd assortment of maternal grandparents. We called my mother's mother, Nana. She was married to 'Uncle Joe,' who was, in fact, no real relative or uncle at all. He was just a nice guy who was Nana's second husband after her divorce from our grandfather. They lived in Bay Shore on Long Island and whenever Nana called on the phone, my mother would roll her eyes and tap her fingernails on the kitchen table.

Lynn and I laughed to think about how Nana always complained about an assortment of illnesses and conditions. She whimpered about everything from her bowels to her headaches. That was usually the topic of telephone conversations and it drove Mom crazy. Nana also had some mental problems in her day and was institutionalized and given electro-convulsive shock treatments for depression. She seemed like a needy soul and was always looking for sympathy. Even at a young age, I could see that she was incapable of being an effective parent to my mother.

Lynn hung a pink, pear-shaped ornament on the tree. "Remember when Nana modeled mink coats for the store?" she asked. Nana worked for many years in Gimbel's Department Store in the fur department.

I nodded and laughed, "And her pictures were in the ads published in all the New York City newspapers." I sashayed across the room, with one hand on my hip, then turned like a model. Lynn laughed and nodded.

I had inherited my love of animals and nature from my Nana. It seemed to me that her occupation of selling and modeling furs was contradictory to love and respect for the animal kingdom. "Hey, Lynn," I hooted, "remember when Mom got ticked off at Nana and told her to stop clanking her false teeth together?" We both began to laugh. "And Nana pouted for hours, until Mom blew up again about her pouting?" By then we were laughing so hard I was worried I would wet my pants. I flopped on the sofa to collect myself. Mom heard the ruckus and came into the room, wiping her hands on her Christmas apron.

"Are you girls letting Jamie and Mikey put some of the decorations on the tree?" she asked as she surveyed the bushy evergreen.

"We certainly are," Lynn lied. The boys were engrossed in a box of tinsel.

Mom reached up and snatched some large ornaments from the top branches, "Well, make sure you put the big ornaments near the bottom and the smaller ones at the top. And let the boys do some."

"I knew we couldn't do it right," my sister whispered to me.

I made a face as my mother left the room and said, "Hey, Lynn, remember the Christmas that Pagar came to visit?"

We called my mother's father Pagar. The second time around he married a flaming redhead, Mickey, who was younger than my mother. Mickey had long red fingernails, wore dresses that showed off her breasts and smelled of expensive perfume. Pagar had black hair that he combed straight back and a thin little mustache. I thought he looked a little like Clark Gable. He always looked dressed up. I was impressed that he wore a belt with his initial on the buckle. A fine silver chain looped from his belt to his pants pocket where a pocket watch was tucked away. It appeared that his priority in life was appearance, and Mickey, 20 years younger and half his age, certainly made him look good.

"Yup, I do remember. Pagar and Mickey drove up in that robin's egg blue Thunderbird." Lynn replied.

"Yes, that was quite the Christmas. Boy, we ate good when they came around." Pagar and Mickey always stopped at a New York deli near their luxury Tudor apartment in Flushing and bought potato salad and delicious cold cuts wrapped in white butcher paper. We feasted on hard salami, German bologna, and cheese that looked like pale yellow lace. The briny dill pickles and Jewish rye bread made lunch quite an experience. The food was delectable and Mom always made a big fuss over it, because as she said, "You can't get real delicatessen food upstate."

"That was the Christmas we got the matching outfits, Lynn. Remember? Those scratchy black and white silk organza dresses, with petticoats underneath?"

Lynn nodded, "And they had bolero jackets that were black velvet and we had black velvet ribbons for our hair. I loved those dresses, but they were so itchy!"

I added, "How about the little kitchen, with the sink that had real running water?" Pagar was big into buying stuff for us. Maybe it was because we were his only two grandchildren, for it was long before Jamie and Mikey were born. Or maybe it was because he was trying to ease guilty feelings for abandoning his daughter at an early age and missing her childhood.

Pagar died of lung cancer when I was 11 years old. I wasn't told he was sick, but I knew something was wrong in the weeks preceding his death when I heard hushed phone conversations and saw my mother's tears. Our parents would not allow my sister or me to go to his funeral on Long Island, even though we asked to go. She and my father left us with the neighbors. So Pagar simply disappeared from our lives.

Now Christmases were fun with Lynn and my little brothers. Mom always made a big deal out of holidays, especially Christmas. She always wore a Christmas apron and danced around the house to the Ray Coniff Singers and Andy Williams records on the stereo. With two little boys in the house, it remained as magical as it was when Lynn and I were young. We counted down days with an advent calendar. We baked almond cookies and hung Dad's boot socks on the wrought iron railing along the stairway. Lynn and I already knew a tangerine, walnuts, and a few small toys would be tucked in the socks on Christmas morning.

Mom always surprised us with gifts we didn't even know we wanted. Like Pagar, she was a generous and creative giver. Every time one of us opened a package, she would have the same remark before the ribbons were even off, "I don't know if you'll like it. If you don't, I saved the receipt. You can exchange it." We always loved whatever she bought us.

For the wages of sin is death, but the gift of God
is eternal life in Christ Jesus our Lord.
Romans 6:23

Chapter 6

I returned to high school in January, excited that I was on the home stretch of my final year of high school. I worked on the yearbook committee and wrote a poem for the yearbook recounting the history of the class of 1968. We decided on a theme for our formal Senior Ball. We would turn the gymnasium into a garden of "Millions of Roses." I was taking fourth year Spanish, art, and science, in addition to English and history. I celebrated my 18th birthday on February 26th, finally old enough to drink alcohol and vote. But neither endeavor was of particular interest to me. I was too busy.

I landed a lead part in the high school spring musical. Mom was so pleased. She cut out every newspaper article and photo of the upcoming show that she could find. She helped me with my costume and offered to help me rehearse my lines. It was good to have an amiable relationship with her. I was grateful for her good-natured kidding and felt like we had finally connected on some level. I was doing something that pleased her immensely.

I studied hard and knew that regents' exams were just around the corner. We ordered graduation caps and gowns and had formal photos taken for the yearbook. "Wear a plain black top and a pearl necklace," the photographer instructed. Boys were to wear a sports jacket, white shirt and tie.

Michael and I were still going steady. "I'm going to marry you someday," he pledged often and sealed his intent with a passionate kiss each time. It appeared that Mom had given up the fight to keep us apart. Michael and I had become very comfortable with each other and even had occasional quarrels, but they never seemed to diminish our love for each other. I spent less and less time with my girlfriends and more and more time with him.

January was cold and snowy and we grew tired of our rides out into the countryside. With the bleak winter landscapes and treacherous roads, we began to park the car in secluded spots just to be alone. Parking was a favorite pastime for teenagers in our town and we didn't see the harm in it. In fact, we giggled when we came upon lovers parked on back roads, with the windows of their cars completely fogged over. But as time went on, our own moral fortitude began to weaken and things began to go too far. It was easy to ignore our sense of morality when we were alone. We deliberately placed ourselves in compromising situations, where we repeatedly had to make decisions to say no to physical intimacy.

But one night we cast our innocence aside and gave ourselves to each other completely. It was a first for both of us. Our world had changed. We were philosophical about the fact that we had saved this amazing and exclusive act for the right person, the person we truly loved. It was not a 'heat of the moment and we lost control' kind of thing. It was a deliberate decision on both our parts. After all, we had talked of marriage several times in the recent past. I didn't feel like I had lost something precious. I felt like we had discovered something sacred. And indeed we had. But the timing was wrong and without the benefit of marriage, our foolish philosophy was deeply flawed.

I knew what the Bible and my parents had to say about sex before marriage. However, I chose to disobey both my earthly and heavenly Father with this carnal transgression. Little did I know that this act of indiscretion would have a long-lasting negative effect on, not only Michael and me, but on a wide circle of our family and friends.

> A gossip betrays a confidence,
> but a trustworthy person keeps a secret.
> Proverb 11:13

Chapter 7

Our only grandson, Nicholas, is visiting from Tennessee. At 16, he has his learners' permit, and I ask him to drive Mike and me to the feed store for grain for the barn animals. I climb into the back and Nick and his Pop occupy the front seats. Nick, a prudent driver, starts the engine and Pop takes the opportunity to give his grandson some unsolicited advice.

"Nick you're a good driver. Now don't make the mistake of becoming over-confident. And don't show off for the girls," he says and pokes Nicholas in the ribs.

"You know what I mean, squealing your tires, slamming on the brakes, or honking the horn needlessly. And no racing. You never know when a cop might be around."

Nick, respectful and tolerant, replies, "OK, Pop." He concentrates on the rear view mirrors as he maneuvers out of our driveway. His grandfather turns to me and winks. I am reminded of Mike's notorious driving habits when he was Nick's age.

*****

As spring arrived, it seemed the teenage boys in town were especially restless. They revved the engines in their old cars to startle the teenage girls walking on the streets. They hooted and hollered out the car windows, as the girls jumped with surprise and smiled back. I met Michael every day in the student parking lot after school so I could catch a ride home with him.

As I hopped into Mike's car one day in late March, he announced we would be attending the drag races on Hardwood Island Road on Friday night. "Cool!" I exclaimed, not knowing exactly what that meant. I was game for anything as long as Mike was with me.

That Friday night as soon as it was dark, we turned onto Hardwood Island Road, a paved seasonal road used in the summer by muck farmers. In March, it stretched out in a straight line across the fertile black mucklands, abandoned until planting season arrived. It was a popular place for lovers to park, but this night there were cars idling along both sides of the road. I recognized many of our friends gathered like pit crews around the cars in the dark. We rolled the windows down as we approached the scene. Someone called, "Hey, Dunny! Are you in?"

Mike parked the car along the road. "Wait here a minute," he instructed and he gave me quick kiss. When he returned, someone standing in the middle of the road motioned us forward. Another car pulled up next to us and the driver revved his engine.

He leaned over, rolled the passenger window down, and shouted, "Dunny, that thing is ready for the scrap heap!"

Mike smiled and threw his cigarette butt out the window. "We're gonna blow your doors off, Buddy!"

All the kids were chanting when someone yelled above the din, "Ready? Set? Go!" My head flew back as Mike gunned the Chevy. We fishtailed down the pavement, both vehicles roaring toward a shadowy figure ahead. Neck and neck, the drivers glanced at each other and then Mike's Chevy surged ahead.

As suddenly as we accelerated, Michael hit the brakes. I braced myself with my hand on the dashboard.

Both guys parked their hotrods in the gravel along the roadside and conferred with the flagman, who was none other than Juggy. He had been standing at the quarter mile finish line. I sat in the car trying to contain my excitement, while the competitors clapped each other on the back good-naturedly and discussed tires and camshafts. I was ready to drag race again. I enjoyed the rush and good-natured competition. Before long, I was hanging out the passenger window, shouting above the commotion, "Ready? Set? Go!"

    Cathy had come to accept my love affair with Michael. I talked incessantly about him and numbered all the wonderful qualities I was discovering about him. She did not have a boyfriend, but I was insensitive to the hurt she must have felt when I prattled on and on about how wonderful it was to have a steady boyfriend.

    I spent most of my free time with Mike, so the only time Cathy and I saw each other was at school. She invited me to football games and shopping, but Michael always took preference over anything else that might be going on. One evening I was invited to spend the night at her house and, with my parents' permission, I walked across town to the big Victorian house where Cathy lived.

    We sat in our pajamas in her room upstairs, globbing Noxzema cream on our faces. Cathy put a Beach Boys album on the record player, turned the volume down a bit and plopped on her bed. "So, what's it really like having a steady boyfriend anyway?" she asked.

I did my best to explain how enamored I was with Michael. "He's the first one on my mind in the morning and I fall asleep thinking about him every night. Cathy, it still feels like there are ping pong balls ricocheting around in my tummy every time I see him!" I said wistfully. "I just want to be with him all the time. Cathy, he wants to marry me," I concluded.

She stared at me a moment, her eyes narrowed, and her nose wrinkled, as though she smelled something unpleasant. "Are you crazy?" she blurted out, obviously not understanding the depth of my romantic involvement with Michael. I continued on, trying to make her realize the seriousness of our bond by revealing more and more details of our relationship. She listened intently and warned, "Jeanne, you shouldn't be so serious about him. What's the matter with you? We're seniors and we'll be leaving for college before you know it. What will you do then?" She sounded amazingly like my mother. Finally, in an attempt to show her the depth of our commitment to each other, I shared the secret of our physical intimacy. As soon as I told her, I knew I had made a mistake. How could I have revealed a secret that belonged only to Michael and me, I asked myself. In the meantime, Cathy was chastising me and expressing her disbelief and disapproval.

"Please, please, don't ever tell anyone!" I begged. "I shouldn't have told you. Promise me you won't breathe a word to anyone?" I knew that I had made a foolish, immature mistake. She agreed to keep the secret to herself. We turned the lights off prematurely to go to sleep, but more so to avoid the awkward atmosphere that suddenly pervaded Cathy's room. Protected by the shadowy darkness, I slipped my thumb into my mouth for the protection and comfort it afforded me. I rubbed my pajama sleeve on my nose. Her bedroom grew silent and in that quiet, I knew a great expanse had formed and separated my friend and me. Things would never be the same between us.

> A gentle answer turns away wrath,
> but a harsh word stirs up anger.
> Proverbs 15:1

Chapter 8

The first Saturday in April I sat on the stairway in the living room watching for Michael from the window at the bottom of the stairs. We had plans to go fishing. I scratched Chipper's ears until dog hair began to drift toward the carpet. Just as Mike turned into the driveway, my mother appeared. "His parents are coming here at one o'clock today. We are going to have a discussion about the two of you," she announced stiffly.

"You called his parents?" I asked in disbelief, "for what?"

"Yes, I did and you both better be here," she concluded, ignoring the second part of my question. Her ominous determination made me uneasy.

Later, Michael and I sat in the shade of a tall cottonwood tree on the shore of Oneida Lake and cast our fishing lines into the green water. We left the car door open and the radio played softly. When the 11 o'clock news came on, the top story was the heartbreaking news that Reverend Martin Luther King had been assassinated. "Jeepers," I said, "First President Kennedy is assassinated and now this."

"The world is falling apart," Mike replied, philosophically, as he stared out over the haze on the lake. Little did we know that our own little world was about to crumble as well.

We were anxious about the impending encounter with all four parents. Having no knowledge of what this summit might be about, we decided to take the opportunity to tell them we wanted to get married. We didn't have a concrete plan, but I was willing to give college a chance if I could marry Michael and attend a college close to home where he could continue to work. We felt this was a good compromise. Our hope was that perhaps if we acted in this responsible manner, we might gain the blessing of both sets of parents. We reeled in our fishing lines, too preoccupied to bother with fishing. As we talked and fretted about the afternoon meeting, our hooks glinted in the sunshine as they dangled at the end of our fishing poles. The fish had taken the bait.

Mr. and Mrs. Dunn arrived at my parents' house shortly after we did. They passed us as we sat on the front steps, where we huddled together in an attempt to gain courage and rehearse our plea. They rang the doorbell and were ushered in. I heard self-introductions between the two sets of parents. We rose, nervously stepped inside, and quietly closed the front door. The Dunn's sat together on the couch. Michael's dad was already calling my father by his first name. "So this weather has been something, huh Jim?" I heard him say. Weather is a safe subject. Everyone must be uncomfortable. My father took a seat in an armchair and my mother perched on the arm of the other chair in the room, as if she were preparing for battle, sitting a bit above all the rest of us. Either that or she was poised for a quick escape, but I doubted that.

Not knowing my place, foolishly, I spoke first, "We have brought you all together today to......" I trailed off, trying to make a joke. No one laughed. I changed my demeanor as I looked from one somber face to another.

My mother spoke, eyeing Mike and me, "You two have put us through just about enough. You don't spend any time with your friends and you're together way too much. We are tired of you two doing just as you damn well please and I'm sure the Dunns are too. So, what do you have to say for yourselves?" I had no idea how to respond.

"Well, we want to get married," Michael began bravely.

My father crossed his arms. "Look here, Jeanne is going to college, so that's not going to happen. You two don't have a clue about what's involved in getting married. And you're both way too young," my father concluded. Mike's parents sat quietly. I was deeply hurt that Dad was obviously taking my mother's side and verbalizing his disapproval of our relationship. I wondered if my generally mellow father had been threatened by my mother that he support her viewpoint or else.

Suddenly, my mother asked the question that blew a hole in the conversation, sending our thoughts and carefully planned dialog crashing out through the windows. She tapped her slippered foot violently on the carpet and glared at the Dunns, "Are you aware that these two have been having sex?" she trumpeted. She had been holding this revelation like a concealed weapon until this moment. Michael and I were shot dead just as surely as if a single bullet had ripped through the both of us.

Michael's folks fidgeted, obviously uncomfortable and surprised. My parents seemed to gain momentum with our silence and shock. Many unkind words were exchanged, including my mother's suggestion that Michael's parents force him to enlist in the service to "get away from her daughter." Mrs. Dunn rightly provoked, shot back, "Why on earth would I do that?" On the evening news, Walter Cronkite reported hundreds of soldiers dying each day in the jungles of Vietnam. How my Mom could say such a heartless thing was beyond my comprehension.

 The law was laid down and Michael and I were told that we were forbidden to see each other alone. "You can see one another in school," was my mother's unsympathetic arrangement. Phone calls would be limited to 15 minutes once a week. I was never to get in his car again. Mike's parents concurred. If any of these edicts were violated, I would be grounded from all activities, including those with my girlfriends. This was my parents' attempt to protect their younger daughter from falling into sinful temptation again. I'm sure they were desperate to safeguard me from an unwanted pregnancy. Most of all, they didn't want me to jeopardize the bright future that they saw ahead for me.

 I hid my face and cried on Michael's shoulder in my parents' living room. I was ashamed and embarrassed that our parents knew. But I could not feel remorse, no matter how far down into my soul I reached. I felt deliriously happy when I was with Michael. He and I had talked about our physical intimacy many times and felt that because we had pledged our love and commitment to each other, we were as good as married. We were wrong. In God's eyes, we were very wrong.

Michael whispered in my ear, "How did they find out?"

"I told Cathy. She must have told my mother," I whimpered in disbelief. I couldn't believe what was happening and it felt like an apocalypse was at hand. In Mike's silence, I knew his mind was reeling as well. Now my parents had a legitimate reason for detesting Michael and objecting to our relationship. This was the first day of a lifetime of anguish and misery for our families. And Michael and I were squarely to blame.

One more cruel remark from Mom, directed at me, ended the visit. "And mark my words, young lady, if a pregnancy occurs that kid will be put up for adoption."

With that, Michael's parents rose to leave. "Let's go, Russell," his mother hissed with distain.

Before leaving, his father stopped to make a point with a rhetorical question. He asked Mike, loudly enough for all to hear, "She's 18, isn't she?" I felt dirty.

A fool spurns a parent's discipline,
but whoever heeds correction shows prudence.
Proverbs 15:5

Chapter 9

Rebecca and I are on the phone, telling her brother, Eric about the genealogy trip we took a few weeks ago. We tell him about the incredible details we uncovered about my father's early days and his family of origin. "No wonder he never shared much!" Eric remarks, "He barely knew his parents or siblings!" We begin to piece together some of the amazing facts we discovered.

*****

Jeanne Wilhite Dunn

January 1928

"*Take it out of your mouth, Johnny,*" *his older brother reprimanded, as he cupped his hand under the two-year-old boy's chin. Jimmy, at four years old, tried to look after his brother as best as he could. Grandmother had suggested Jimmy mind his brother by playing marbles in the alley between their apartment house and the paper box company building next door. There was no snow in the alleyway, but the cold January air was creeping through the children's thin coats. Johnny spit the wet aggie into Jimmy's hand. Jimmy picked up the rest of his marbles and the piece of string that Pa had given him. His father, Hoyt Wilhite, worked around the corner as a cook at the Coney Island Lunch Room in Quincy, Illinois. He had brought the string home to Jimmy and explained how the bags of flour arriving daily at the back of the restaurant were sewn closed with string.*

The winter sun was just beginning to touch the horizon across the Mississippi River. Soon it would be dark. Jimmy loved to wander to the great river's edge to play in the mud at the end of Vermont Street. He spent hours watching the barges and steamboats as they floated up and down the river, cutting through the smooth, muddy water. But Grandmother, who had been staying with them, had said, "Don't you dare go down there, Jimmy." She was in charge now. Mama had said so when she first got sick. Grandmother was too busy looking after Mama and the new baby to take Jimmy to the river. Before Mama took sick, she walked Jimmy and Johnny to the river almost every day. But now his mother moaned and tossed in her bed while Grandmother wiped the sweat off her face with a towel. In fact, Mama had remained in bed ever since his baby brother, George Gordon was born, three weeks ago.

Jimmy brushed the dust off his younger brother's hands and the two headed inside. Grandmother had promised earlier in the day that she would make 'panny cakes' for dinner. Jimmy and Johnny were hungry, dirty and cold, but there would be no dinner tonight.

The doctor, who had come to look after Mama several times before, bent over his black bag, "I'm so sorry," he muttered, shaking his head sadly. He avoided looking at the boys as they entered the dark, cramped apartment.

Grandmother's eyes were red-rimmed and she blew her nose into a yellow hankie. "Yer Ma's gone," she said to the boys, sniffing.

Jimmy was confused, "But I thought she was sick! What do you mean? Gone where, Grandmother?" Grandmother shook her head and turned her back to the children. Pa stood at the kitchen window over the sink and stared out into the darkness settling over Quincy. He leaned heavily on his hands, which were positioned on either side of the sour-smelling sink. Blue cigarette smoke coiled like a serpent from the fingers on his right hand.

Helen Louise Pritchett Wilhite, was 19 years old when puerperal fever took her life. A devastating disease, it affected women within the first three days after childbirth and progressed rapidly, causing severe abdominal pain and fever. Helen's three young sons were placed in an orphanage within days of her death. Their grandmother, Mary Ellen Pritchett, lived with her 8-year-old son, William, in a tiny apartment on the riverfront and was unable to take the children after her daughter's death. Baby George died of pneumonia three months after his mother's death and Jimmy and John never saw each other again. Hoyt Lane Wilhite, mysteriously disappeared shortly after his wife's premature death, never to see his sons again.

Jimmy was my father. When he was older, he crossed his beloved Mississippi River and wandered alone from farm to farm across Missouri throughout his teenage years. We found his name on old census records, listed as a common laborer or farm hand. Times were hard in the 1930's in the Midwest and farmers offered my father a roof over his head and meals in exchange for his hard work. As soon as the armed services would take him, with no family and no ties, he joined the US Coast Guard to help the World War II effort. I'm sure his motivation for selecting that particular branch of the armed services was his lifelong love of seagoing vessels, a love that began on the mighty Mississippi River.

*****

"Jeanne, hand me that wrench." My father's voice startled me. He held out his hand without looking up. In the basement, I held a trouble light for hours on end while my father worked on his Fiat. I always felt that I had an alliance with my dad and it bothered me to be out of his good graces.

"Daddy, my hands are getting cold. It's so chilly down here," I complained.

"Alright then, go on. Go see what your mother has for you to do." I laid the trouble light down on the fender of the car and scampered up the basement stairs. As he carefully propped the light to illuminate his work area, he called, "Thanks, Jeanne."

After the big parental meeting, my parents informed me that they would keep me busy working around the house, instead of pining over Michael. And indeed they did. From the time I got home from school, there were lists and directives for a multitude of chores. I did laundry, including ironing the entire family's clothes. I scrubbed floors, washed windows, and vacuumed. Mike and I began writing letters almost daily once my sentence started. Neither one of us had much of anything to say, but we wrote how much we loved and missed each other.

"I'm done helping Dad," I called. My mother put me to work. I mowed the lawn and weeded under the rosebushes until my arms bled. I sat back, my knees bent under me, examining the scratches from the thorns. I admired the pale pink roses that covered the bushes. I thought idly about how lovely and fragrant the blooms were, and how God had surrounded them with sharp thorns. It seemed to symbolize my relationship with Michael. I had to struggle through the thorns to get to the beauty and splendor of my beau.

My parents were curt when they spoke to me and made it clear that they were angry with me. I wrote to Mike and described what I felt was inhumane treatment at home. He wrote back, "Just do whatever they say and don't talk back. They can't make us stop loving each other." He was wise beyond his years and more mature than most men.

So I did as I was told. On the weekends, I babysat for my little brothers. Jamie was born when I was 14 and Mikey was born two years later, so I was the in-house babysitter. I loved my little brothers and didn't mind at all. I was surprised that my parents trusted that I would not invite Mike to stop by in their absence. But they only stayed away for a few hours at a time. I wished my sister were home, instead of living, what I determined to be, a life of exotic travel and adventure. At least I would have one alliance and someone to talk to in the house.

After two weeks of hard labor and the cold shoulder, I was tired of the routine. Mom arrived home with groceries and dropped into a kitchen chair. While I put the groceries away, I nonchalantly mentioned the upcoming Senior Ball, "Mom, can I tell the committee I will help with decorating the gym? The theme is "Millions of Roses," you know, the song by Steve Lawrence," I ventured. I moved the Wyler's Drink Mix packages in the cupboard over the toaster to make room for the jar of Nescafe instant coffee, my father's favorite.

"I suppose," was the curt answer.

Encouraged, I asked, "Can I go to the ball?" I paused and took a deep breath, "with Michael?" I continued my work to hide my anxiety and did not look at Mom. I threw a box of Neapolitan ice cream into the freezer compartment of the refrigerator and turned. My mother fixed her eyes on me, pondering, while Jamie banged a Fisher Price school bus in her lap.

"I'll talk to your father about it," she said. I was ecstatic. It was better than a flat out 'no.'

Little by little, Mike and I devised ways to see each other, despite my parents' rules. In school, we walked to classes together. After school, I met him in the student parking lot for quick conversations and kisses. I was walking home from school again, but one day I saw Mike slowly approaching me several blocks from my house. He stopped the car beside me and smiled, "Do you dare to get in?" I looked up and down the street and jumped in his car. From then on, he drove me from school to Hickory Street every day. I walked the rest of the way home and assumed my parents would never know the difference. Not only was I disobedient, but sneaky too.

Many are the plans in a person's heart,
but it is the Lord's purpose that prevails
Proverbs 19:21

Chapter 10

We have a single photograph of the one time Michael and I went to a formal high school dance. If I look closely, I can see a few blemishes on my face. Michael's skin is radiant and he looks tan. I chuckle when I think how, even today, people ask if we've been in the Caribbean again when they see his dark skin. "It's his Italian and Irish Heritage," I laugh.

As I stare at the details of the photo, I reminisce about the dismal circumstances the night of our Senior Ball. It's been 47 years, but I can remember the instant my father clicked the camera like it was yesterday. Once again, I feel the surge of emotions from that night.

*****

When my parents gave me permission to attend the Senior Ball with Michael, I felt a twinge of guilt because of the devious encounters we had executed. But I supposed their lack of resolve meant they weren't really serious about keeping Mike and me apart.

Mom brought me to her hairdresser the morning of the dance. My hair was teased, swept up into a blonde bubble and some large curls arranged on top of my head. We tucked tiny paper rosebuds into each curl. Later in the day, I dressed for the dance in my room and felt like a princess when I glided down the stairs into the living room. I wore a dress my mother borrowed from a friend whose daughter was now in college. The skirt was white and the bodice was avocado green, overlaid with white lace in a daisy pattern. The dress had an empire waist and was sleeveless. As always, I had no choice in what I would wear. But I didn't care. I was going to the Senior Ball with Michael.

My mom finished zipping up the back of the dress and said, "Come with me." She led me into my parents' bathroom downstairs. My floor-length gown rustled with each step I took. She offered her make-up bag and showed me how to put on rouge and mascara. With a spritz of her Lily of the Valley cologne, I was ready.

"You look beautiful, Babe," she said.

I kissed her cheek. "Love you, Mom." It was a spontaneous kiss. I wanted her to know that I appreciated and loved her, especially at that moment. I knew how much she loved me. She showed it in so many ways. But I was always looking at the negative, the times she scolded me or restricted me. It didn't occur to me that her constraints might be to protect me.

Michael rang the doorbell and I jumped. As I opened the door, my heart felt as though it would spring from my chest. He was dressed in a tuxedo, black pants, white jacket, and black bowtie. His thick dark hair was combed carefully into place and his face shone. He smiled and winked but did not speak. He handed me a pink box that contained a bouquet of flowers. The yellow Shasta daisies and baby's breath were tied with green satin ribbons that matched the bodice of my dress. I ran to the refrigerator to retrieve the yellow carnation for Michael's lapel. As I fumbled to pin the flower on Michael's jacket,

I thought about how much courage it must have taken for him to come to the door.

"Jim, get the camera," my mother instructed. He took one photo of Michael and me smiling into each other's faces in front of the wrought iron banister in our living room.

I had told Michael that my parents were only allowing me to go to the dance. We were only to drive to and from the school and nowhere else. We were not permitted to go out after the dance for dinner, as was the custom, and I was to be home by 11:00 pm. While neither of us was happy with the constraints, we were thrilled that we had a few precious hours together.

Before we left for the dance, my father said sternly, "She's to be home by 11 o'clock." Mike nodded and we left.

We danced to the slow songs at the ball, but sat on the sidelines and talked while the rest of the kids gyrated on the dance floor, doing the twist and the pony. By now, everyone in our graduating class knew that we were a committed couple. They stopped to ask what plans we had after graduation. They teased, "Marriage, right?" Mike and I just smiled and avoided answering. We had no idea what the future held for us. When Herb Alpert sang, "This Guy's in Love with You," Mike pulled me onto the dance floor. We embraced and sang the lyrics to each other, rocking gently, pretending to dance. The night ended much too quickly. The rest of the kids left the gymnasium to go to fancy restaurants for dinner and on to home parties after that. They wouldn't be home until the wee hours of the morning. Michael and I left so I would be home by the 11:00 curfew. My past disobedience, lying and insolence caused mistrust and its consequences.

Jeanne Wilhite Dunn

> He who began a good work in you will carry it
> on to completion until the day of Christ Jesus.
> Philippians 1:6

Chapter 11

The morning of graduation day I was up early enough to hear the birds awaken and begin their chitchat in the branches of the white birch outside my bedroom window. I was excited, but somewhere deep inside a little splinter of unease jabbed at me. I pondered the feeling while I dressed for the day. I slipped into the white cotton shift dress I had sewn myself. I had selected white fabric embroidered all over with tiny red rosebuds and spent hours listening to the drone of Mom's sewing machine as I finished my creation.

At 8:30 I took my burgundy cap and gown off the hook on my bedroom door and bounced down the stairs. Dad returned with the babysitter for Jamie and Mikey and I noticed he was wearing dress pants and a rust-colored sports jacket. He rarely got dressed up and I was pleased and thankful that this was apparently, an important day for him too. "Everyone ready?" Mom chirped, and we left for the high school. My parents took seats in the auditorium and I joined my graduating class in the gym. There our class advisors positioned us in alphabetical order. I searched the crowd of just over 100 students for Michael. He spotted me and waved from near the front of the line. With the last name of Wilhite, I was accustomed to being nearly last for everything.

Our class advisors escorted us to the auditorium, where we paraded down the two center aisles and took our seats in front while "Pomp and Circumstance" played on a tinny-sounding turntable somewhere. So both Michael and I officially graduated from Canastota High School that sunny day. After the ceremony families and graduates were reunited in jubilant and noisy confusion. I was still forbidden to see or interact with Mike and lost sight of him quickly. This seemed rather ridiculous when we had been allowed to go to the Senior Ball just a week prior. I searched for a glimpse of my boyfriend as my father snapped photos of me, squinting in the bright sunshine outside. "Can I take my cap and gown off now," I grumbled, suddenly downhearted. Now that I was formally done with high school, I faced the ongoing crusade to find my way into Michael's arms forever. Simply graduating from high school seemed anticlimactic. My parents were still bitter and I was not allowed to attend any of my friends' graduation parties.

There was no party for me, but my parents invited their best friends to join us for lunch on the back patio. The couple brought me a graduation gift, a small, blue hobnail vase. I saw it as a start to my trousseau. My parents gave me a tiny gold typewriter for my charm bracelet. We ate hamburgers and potato salad. No one said much and the meager conversation was guarded.

I retreated to my room after lunch and could hear remnants of the conversation on the patio below. The adults seemed much more relaxed and chatted happily. I have become the proverbial elephant in the room, I thought as my thumb found its way to my mouth once again. At least I had stopped wetting the bed, since Michael came into my life. I rubbed the hem of my pillow case on my nose. 'Shommy' is what our family called my thumb-sucking habit when I was a little girl. Now that I was 18 and a high school graduate, it was called repulsive.

Where Once There Were Thorns

> Show me the way I should go,
> for to you I lift up my soul.
> Psalm 143:8

Chapter 12

Today I stop to pick up some shrimp and vegetables for our dinner tonight. As I put my grocery items on the conveyer belt, they suddenly lurch forward and glide out of my reach. I scoot up to the cashier and hear the bleep, bleep, bleep as she drags each item over a small glass plate. She announces the total, $42.05. I contemplate giving her a fifty-dollar bill and a nickel, but decide against it. I don't want to put her on the spot, considering cashiers can't seem to count back change these days. I am getting old and cynical. I think back to when I was a cashier, my first real job. We didn't have *any conveyer belts. And I thought I knew everything. At least I knew how to count back change at Ira's P & C Market.*

*****

By the Fourth of July, I was restless. Because school was over, opportunities to see Michael were rare. The constant chore lists had dwindled and my parents appeared to have forgiven me, but I wasn't naive enough to think they had forgotten. The outrage displayed at the parents' meeting began to subside some. I felt like the subject of a family scandal and I hated the fact that they were so deeply disappointed in me.

At my mother's urging, I got a job at the local grocery store, Ira's P & C Market, as a cashier. I enjoyed it very much and found I was good at ringing up groceries, redeeming coupons, and handing out the green stamps the store offered.

I felt rather pompous that I could push the right buttons on the cash register without even looking. I couldn't look since I was busy reaching for the items on the counter. The cash register did not calculate change, but I knew how to make change and count it back to the customer. And I was an expert bagger. I could snap open the brown bag, keep one hand inside to receive and position the stuff, and use the other hand to gently toss the grocery items in. I enjoyed the part-time work and made friends with the other employees. "You'd better save up some money for college," my parents hounded.

The college 'selection' started in my junior year of high school, long before Michael and I met. Our family assumed that I would attend college after high school. Lynn's flight attendant career had ended and she was attending the State University at Brockport, in western New York State. When it came time to select a college for me, my parents had already made the choice. There was no need to look at other colleges. I would attend Brockport so my sister and I could make the 2-hour trip there and back home together. We would be in the same place, which would make life much simpler for all of us.

I was envious of my friends, whose parents were taking them all over New York State to look at different campuses before they made their decisions. "I really like Brockport the best," I lied, so no one would know that for me, there were no other options to explore. I was accepted at Brockport and when it came time to declare a major, my mother persuaded me to study theater arts.

I thought back to my participation in the high school musical production. Big glossy black and white photographs of me and others in the cast were posted about town. The local newspaper, the "Bee Journal," ran a few feature stories about the musical and photos of the cast. My mother often told my sister and me that she had aspired to be a dancer and performer on stage, so my brief stardom pleased her on many levels. What about the four years of math, science, and foreign language I took in high school? Maybe I wanted to become a veterinarian or a lawyer. But the choice had been made and I was too naïve to even dream of challenging it. It did occur to me though, that my mom was living vicariously through me.

When Mike and I began dating in the fall of our senior year, I began to look upon leaving for college in a completely different light. As we became more serious about our relationship, I knew college was going to be an issue.

Michael got very little support or encouragement from his parents to continue his education after high school. His father's mantra was, "You're going to be in jail by the time you're 18." So we both knew that Michael would stay in Canastota and pursue the best job he could find and I would go on to college. When we were alone, I whispered in Michael's ear, "I don't want to go to college. I don't want to leave you." But at home, not wanting to dash my parents' dreams or cause an argument, I quietly waited. I didn't have the courage to express to them how I felt.

Michael's part time well-drilling job became full time after graduation. He was out in the field often, but when he could, he came to the store to visit me during lunch breaks. One day my mother came to the break room in the back of the store and found us chatting together. It was as if a bandage had suddenly been ripped off the injured bond between my mom and me. It had been trying to heal, but now our relationship would suffer anew. My mother was furious.

When I got home that day, she was waiting. Her words were venomous, "I thought we made it clear that you are NOT to see that boy. I will do whatever I have to, to keep that bastard away from you. For God's sake, you're going to college soon and you'll forget all about him. Can't you see that?"

"No, that's not true." I screamed, indignant that she would assume such a thing.

"If I find out that you have seen him again, anywhere or anytime, we will put you in a foster home. You have put your father and I through enough hell! Don't defy me again!" she shrieked. She threw a wire hanger into the hall closet, slammed the door shut and spun around. We stood face to face in the hallway and time stopped. My small brothers abandoned their GI Joe figures and stood fearfully in the kitchen watching us.

It felt like something in my mind detonated and the blast spewed from my lips, "I hate you! I hate you!" I bellowed. A primal, frustrated screech followed. Was that me? My voice sounded as though it belonged to someone else, a demon, and it terrified me. I wanted to punch my mother and it took every bit of willpower I had to control myself. I turned and ran toward my room in tears. Before I started up the stairs she further antagonized me. She lowered her voice and hardheartedly told me to make my choice-Michael or my family. It seemed that nothing would ever change her deep resentment of the boy I loved.

I rolled back and forth on my bed with my fists clenched in anguish. I sobbed and cursed my mother under my breath. Screaming into my pillow, I begged a God I didn't know, to free me from the terrible mess I had made of my life. One moment I felt deep regret for having told my mother I hated her. In the next, I was furious that she thought I could just forget Michael. I lay on my bed until I had no more tears to shed. I turned to face the wall and slipped my thumb in my mouth. I cradled it there in the curve of my tongue and rubbed the hem of my top sheet on my nostrils until I fell asleep.

A few weeks later I had another particularly ugly argument with my mother. That night I was unable to sleep and wondered how my life had been reduced to rubble. My teenage angst was like a horrible chronic disease. When I tried to do what was right and good, no one seemed to notice, but if I messed up, everyone, including the neighbors, knew about it. My parents accused me of making life miserable for both them and my little brothers. I answered them with contempt, reminding them, "I am 18 and I can do what I want."

"That's right," my mother shouted, "But as long as you live under our roof, you will do as we say!"

"I am not a baby anymore!" I sneered. When I actually verbalized it, the concept suddenly became real to me. I was depressed and miserable. And I *was* making the rest of the family miserable. I formulated a plan. I dozed but watched the neon green hands of the alarm clock next to my bed. I rose quietly at midnight. Everyone in the family slumbered in the darkness. I dressed in silence, threw on a sweater, and tiptoed down the stairs. I held my breathe as I unlocked the front door. Click. No one stirred. I slipped out into the cool night air. I took a deep cleansing breath as I slowly and carefully closed the door behind me. Then I ran as fast as I could out into the night. The inky darkness felt good. I began to gain control and dominion over my thoughts and emotions. I knew exactly where I was headed.

I ran through the village streets and did not slow my pace until I crossed the bridge over the Interstate

Highway 90 on the edge of town. The world was quiet except for the cacophony of nocturnal insects singing their songs in the shadows. I headed out toward the muck- lands and passed Hardwood Island Road. As I continued out into the country, the darkness swallowed me up. I could barely see the pavement and I strained my eyes to follow the white line along the side of the road. I walked for nearly 2 hours. Two cars approached during the night and I hid in the deep ditches on the side of the road until they passed and were out of sight. Oddly, there was no fear or regret as I traveled. My mind was focused on my love for Michael and with each step, my emotions calmed and my thoughts became clear. The world slept while I gained momentum and took control of my destiny.

When I arrived at Michael's house, I knew he would be the only one there. His parents owned a tavern in a neighboring town and lived upstairs there, along with his younger sister. It was too much of a drive for them to live home and travel there daily. So at 18 years old, Michael rattled around alone in the house in which he grew up.

In the shadows, I found Mike's Chevy parked by the barn. I climbed into the familiar space of his car, curled up on the front seat and tried to sleep until sunrise. Michael worked long hours at his job and I hated to wake him, but at daybreak, I knocked loudly on the front door. I waited. He opened the door slowly, rubbing his head and squinting at me. "What are you doing?" he asked, then opened the door wider.

"I ran away," I announced, as I slipped inside. "I can't stand to live there anymore, Michael. Please, can you help me?"

He was wide-awake now, his rational mind active again. He began a query, "Why'd you do that? How did you get here? What about your job?" He ended with a proclamation, "Jeanne, come on! This is crazy!"

I shrugged and countered, "Well, I am not going back."

"Jeepers Creepers," he said and I thought I heard disappointment in his voice. "Let me get dressed." He disappeared and I wandered through the living room. Stinky ashtrays were full of white cigarette butts, smashed down on their ashen heads like tiny crumpled accordions. I noticed that there were no family photos on display and thought absent-mindedly that perhaps the Dunns did not own a camera. My parents had many photos of their four children. A tangle of Michael's clean clothes sat in a pink plastic laundry basket at the bottom of the stairs.

I jumped when he reappeared, "Just give me a minute," he said. I heard water running in the bathroom and familiar sounds of a morning routine. I recognized the muffled sounds of Mike brushing his teeth and gargling. I smiled. I longed to be a part of those everyday moments with him. I wanted to share my life with the man I loved.

He reappeared and in business-like fashion said, "OK, let's go." I wondered where we might be going, but followed him out the door. Once in his car, we sat and talked for a long time.

"You'd better go back home."

"No, Michael. They are so mean. I want to be able to see you," I wailed.

"Jeanne, they are probably calling the cops right now to report you're missing."

"No they aren't. They don't care about me. All they care about is making me miserable."

"How about if I go back with you? We'll try talking to your parents. And what about your job?" He was so pragmatic it was maddening.

"No, I am not going back. I don't care if I have to live in a cave." I finally convinced him that I did not intend to return home. He had a friend whose sister rented a small apartment in nearby Oneida. She agreed to allow me to stay there, since she was often away on business.

Later that day, I mustered all my courage and went back to Stroud Street to get my things. As Michael drove up to the house, I noticed Mom was pushing Jamie and Mikey on the swing set in the backyard. When Dad heard the front door open, he emerged from the kitchen, coffee cup in hand. Before either of us could say a word, my mother appeared.

"I've come to get some clothes. I am going to stay with a friend," I said hoarsely.

I turned to head upstairs and my mother softly replied acquiescently, "OK, have it your way." I did not look back.

"We all need a break." I said awkwardly. I climbed the stairs and quickly grabbed up a few articles of clothing and my toothbrush. I walked back down stairs, physically shaking. No one spoke. The silence was no longer charged with the likelihood of harsh words. It was simply a vacuum.

I spent the rest of the summer in that wretched smelly apartment. Every morning I took the bus back to Canastota to work at the grocery store and returned in the evening, tired and depressed. It was my choosing to leave the comforts of home on Stroud Street and it didn't take long to regret my decision. Life was not so rosy on my own, especially when I came down with a terrible cold and sore throat. I lay on the sofa that smelled like mildew and suffered with what felt like razor blades in my throat. It hurt to breathe and fever caused me to have horrible dreams. Michael came by and offered over-the-counter cold remedies, but I missed my mom calling me "Babe" and making things better. As soon as I was well again, I asked my parents if I could come home. They allowed me to return. College was only two weeks away. I had only been living on my own for three weeks, but it seemed like forever.

> He who finds a wife finds what is good
> and receives favor from the Lord.
> Proverbs 18:22

Chapter 13

In late August of 1968, I arrived at the State University at Brockport. I moved into one of the new high-rise dorms at the edge of the campus. Since Lynn was a senior, she lived in off-campus housing with friends. Mom and Dad helped me move into the dorm and Mom chattered about how I should attend social events and meet other people. It was clear to me she intended for me to meet and start dating 'college men' who would make lots of money and wear 3-piece suits to work when they began their corporate careers after college. Even at the age of 18, I knew in my heart that her shallow criteria for suitable men were not anything that I was even remotely concerned about. "Have fun, Babe," were my mother's parting words. Perhaps 'study hard' would have been more appropriate, but I had become proficient at reading the hidden messages in her words. Just before she left, Mom instructed me to go to the college library where I would have a paying job a few hours a week as a page. I had no idea that she had arranged this. As soon as my parents left to return home, I pinned up photos of Michael on my bulletin board.

I made friends quickly with the other 5 girls in my suite. I told them all about how Michael and I planned to marry someday soon. They were mesmerized when I told them how in love we were. They were there to get degrees but nevertheless, our romance captivated them. I was simply there to please my parents.

The first Friday night at school, one of my roommates offered to pierce my ears. I thought it sounded like a great idea. We all sang loudly and with heart along with the Beatles as they crooned "Hey Jude" on the record player. Mary numbed my ear lobes with a large ice cube and then, using the biggest safety pin I had ever seen, she plunged it into my earlobe. I heard the crunch of cartilage and sang louder. The following week I cut my hair in a radical style, short, cut around the ear on one side and longer and one length on the other. The haircut showed off my newly pierced ears. I tried my best to shake off the traditions of the home life I had come to despise. I had already forgotten how good it was to return home after my stay in that dreadful apartment. I tried to shape my own destiny and identity by first changing my appearance.

The first week of classes was stifling with the heat of late August. I sat in the fifth floor window staring down at the vast parking lot and missed Michael. Everyone had left for the free Gordon Lightfoot concert in the quad. At that time I had no idea who he was and declined the invitation to go. Michael called every night at the same time and my roommates knew to let me answer the 8 pm phone calls, but I missed his presence.

Every Sunday he made the 4-hour round trip to visit. He was working two jobs, pumping gas in the evening and working with the well-drilling crew during the day. Sundays were his only day off. I sat in the window watching for him and went flying and tripping down five flights in the stairwell when I saw his car. I was a sentinel at my post on the fifth floor of Perry Hall. I watched every Sunday for the 1963 Chevy Super Sport convertible with a turquoise interior. He retired the old car we had dated in and purchased this more dependable and classy means of transportation.

Every Sunday Mike bought subs and sodas and we ate outdoors or in the safety of his car when the weather was bad. Harrison Dining Hall was closed on Sundays and the college students had to fend for themselves. We window-shopped along Main Street in Brockport or drove to the apple and peach orchards just outside of town. Just being together was enough for both of us. As soon as I was in his arms, I felt like I was whole again. We talked, schemed, dreamed and huddled together and silently worried what the future held for us. I cried every time we had to say goodbye.

I certainly did not make the most of my time in college at Brockport. At first, I attended classes and although I didn't listen to the lectures, I did try to read the required material. Any other time, classes in theater arts, psychology and history would have been of interest to me, but the only thing I could think of was how much I missed Michael.

Inevitably, I found myself studying Good Housekeeping magazines instead of taking notes from the heavy "Introduction to Theater" textbook. I cut out photos and copied recipes. I made lists of things we would need for our household and lists of baby names. I wanted to be a wife and mother. I read bridal magazines and scrutinized wedding gowns and flower arrangements. Slowly I began to admit to myself that I could no longer relinquish my hopes and dreams. Throughout that first semester at college, I became more and more grounded in my convictions. Eventually, I simply stopped attending classes.

I was soon to learn that Michael's heart was in the same place. One Sunday in early November, I watched as he drove into the parking lot. I slid the window open as far as I could, enough to get my arm out and waved joyfully. He stepped out of his car and held up a small object for me to see. Looking up he shouted, "Jeanne, will you marry me?" I loved the elegant solitaire diamond ring he had chosen to seal our commitment to each other. I was officially engaged! I felt like the world around me was suddenly enchanted.

We wrote letters to each other almost daily and reassured one another of our faithfulness to our relationship. In our immaturity, we both had trust issues and clung to each other desperately. I wrote of the funny escapades that occurred in our dorm and Michael sent me news about his work. In our letters, Michael and I discussed how to proceed into the future. I suggested that we drive to another state and elope. I told him I had saved $100 from the work-study job at the college library. Michael decided that it was unwise to travel so far from home to get married. It sounded like a romantic thing to do, but Mike was too level-headed to concur.

"Besides, where would we live?" my sensible fiancée pointed out. We wanted to be married in a church. So we decided against running off to get married. Thank God one of us was sensible. But we were committed and decided we would get married as soon as possible. Love was a powerful thing. Waiting just wasn't an option anymore.

*Delight yourself in the Lord,
and he will give you the desires of your heart.
Psalm 37:4*

Chapter 14

My roommate Mary and I went shopping in nearby Greece Town Mall the following Saturday. It was an especially cold November day when we piled into her green Volkswagen bug. I kicked my way into the tiny car, stepping on a SkyBar and several Hostess Snowball wrappers on the floor. A Baby Ruth candy bar wrapper stuck to the bottom of my left boot. Mary twisted the volume knob on the flat dashboard and Otis Reading's "Sittin' on the Dock of the Bay" filled the small car. Mary pounded out the rhythm on the steering wheel and we both sang the lyrics. I rubbed my hands together and blew my warm breath on them, and wished the VW had a better heater.

We passed a lovely Cape Cod house and suddenly I stopped singing. The house looked very much like the house my parents had built on Stroud Street. I thought of Mom and Dad. How I wished it were my Mom I was shopping with this day. Why can't things be different, I lamented. I wondered if Mom had a friend to accompany her when she got her wedding dress. I thought about my mother's wedding. She never got the chance to wear a beautiful, formal wedding gown. I thought about the rest of the story of my parents' romance and marriage.

The courtship lasted only 60 days and my parents were married on July 7, 1945 at the Washington Square Methodist Church, just a block west of the arch that marked their first encounter.

Dad wore the best clothing he had, his dress white Coast Guard uniform and my mother wore a two-piece light blue dress. The only witnesses present, as recorded on the marriage certificate, were Mom's lifelong best friend, Alyce Hofmann, who also lived at St Christopher's Boarding School and a fellow sailor friend of my Dad's at the time. After they wed, my father returned to active duty aboard the USS Knoxville, and my mother went to live with her Aunt Chris in Queens. A letter writing frenzy ensued, as the newlyweds confessed their love and began to learn more about each other. Five months later on December 20, 1945, Jim, a USCG Fireman, First Class, received his honorable discharge. He was 21 years old, my mother 17. By this time, they were awaiting the arrival of their first child, my sister, due in April 1946.

I twisted my beautiful diamond ring around my finger and my stomach lurched. What will my parents say when they see this? Should I hide it when I go home for Thanksgiving? Mary jerked me back to the present, slamming on her brakes. "Whoops, I almost missed the mall," she laughed and swerved into the parking lot.

Mary had agreed to help me shop for a wedding gown. I was grateful since she shared my enthusiasm and seemed genuinely happy for me. I knew specialty stores and wedding boutiques would be too expensive, so we decided to check out Sibley's, a popular, upscale department store. I knew Sibley's had a cozy niche where several racks of wedding gowns and prom dresses were on display.

A rather prim sales clerk approached as we fingered the sleeve of a beaded white gown. "And who is the bride to be?" she asked with an almost imperceptible bit of arrogance. "She is," replied Mary, shoving me forward. The sales clerk brought her hands up in front of her chest and interlaced her white, bony fingers. She shifted her gaze toward me.

Suddenly I felt inept. "Yes, I am," I squeaked, wondering if she heard the hesitation in my voice. At that moment, it seemed like I was pretending, participating in my own made-up fairy tale. Was I even mature enough to get married? At 18, was I prepared to interact like an adult with this silver-haired prude? I wanted my thumb desperately, but knew how absurd the impulse was.

Mary spoke up when she sensed my dry mouth and shrinking courage, "We just want to browse a bit." Thankfully, the sales clerk nodded and moved away from us. "Check out that hair," Mary whispered sarcastically. "She looks like a *very* old Madame Butterfly." The sales clerk's hair was pulled back so severely into a French twist that it made her eyes look like a geisha girl. We both tittered, like insensitive teens, instead of mature college women. I was ashamed of myself, but I laughed anyway.

I picked out three gowns from a circular rack with a sign that read, "50% off." These were leftover winter gowns that Sibley's needed to move to make room for the spring and summer stock. Most brides-to-be bought wedding dresses months and months before their wedding day. I tiptoed into the fitting room, tripping on the heavy load in my arms.

Mary settled into a plush chair and said, "Okay girl, let's see what you've got!" The second gown I tried on fit perfectly and when I stepped up on the pedestal in front of the 3-way mirrors, I knew this was my wedding dress. It was very simple but elegant and I loved it. I twisted my arm to see the price tag. It was on sale for $75.00. It was white velvet as soft and warm as a pony's nostrils. The simple round neck and long sleeves were trimmed in heavy Venetian lace. The long velvet train was edged with the same lace. Remarkably, it fit like a glove.

"This is it!" I told Mary. She nodded her head vigorously and dabbed at the tears in her eyes. When she grabbed a headpiece and pinned it on my head with a cathedral length veil attached to it, I started to cry. Never in my life had I felt so beautiful. I turned from left to right, admiring the simple but dramatic train of white velvet. I was overwhelmed and speechless. I put it on layaway with a deposit of $15.00. In my mind that dress would always be my wedding gown even though I would never wear it.

Thanksgiving was an uneventful holiday at home, primarily because I kept my beautiful diamond engagement ring hidden from view. I did not yet have the courage to face the consequences of what its revelation would bring. We all watched the Macy's Thanksgiving

Day parade on TV. Jamie sat on my lap and wiggled with excitement. Lynn bounced Mikey on her knee. Later we ate turkey and Dad's favorite, homemade cranberry sauce with whole cranberries in it. Mom's food was delicious, as always, the conversation around the table was bland. We were all polite and careful not to say anything that might ruin the holiday. Weather was, as usual, a popular topic of conversation over pumpkin pie.

    The Christmas season arrived in 1968 with the usual fanfare. Lynn and I stumbled up the front steps laden down with laundry, shoes and books.

    "Hi Mom! Hi Dad," I called as we shoved our way through the front door. We dropped our things and gave our parents and brothers hugs. I had my engagement ring on and glanced at it over my dad's shoulder as I embraced him. I knew I had to muster my courage, wear the ring, and tell my parents about our engagement. It was childish and irresponsible to try to hide it any longer. I walked into the kitchen and called, "Mom, I have something to show you. Can you come in here for a minute?" I took a deep shaky breath. I sat down at the kitchen table and casually extended my left hand. She looked at the diamond ring and then at me. I smiled. Much to my surprise, she did not appear angry, but rather unperturbed. "Isn't it beautiful?" I asked. She looked at it closely, moving the ring a bit on my finger to watch the diamond sparkle. I wondered if she was thinking about the fact that she never had a diamond engagement ring.

"Very beautiful," she said and took her time examining it. Finally she spoke, "Jeanne, do you want some tea?" As she moved away from the table to put the teakettle on, I was pleased that her compliment had seemed genuine and sincere. Lynn joined us in the kitchen and the three of us chatted easily about school, the hometown football team, Christmas, everything, except Michael.

Later, I found my father and sat down next to him on the couch. "Hi Daddy," I ventured. He folded his newspaper neatly and deliberately. I placed my left hand on his knee and stretched my fingers out.

He eyed my engagement ring and said, "Has your mom seen that yet?"

"Yup, I showed her earlier. What do you think, Dad?" I wanted him to hug me and congratulate me. I wanted him to express his happiness and support. But he simply shook his head in resignation and sighed. My family seemed to focus on the ring itself as a lovely piece of jewelry and not so much on what it symbolized. But the only sparks that flew that Christmas were from the big stone fireplace my father had built at one end of the living room. For me, that was cause enough for celebration in my heart, but I was wary. The atmosphere still seemed tainted with oppression.

Lynn had a boyfriend now, Jack, who was quite handsome and charming. He had an intellectual air about him, tall, well spoken, with horn-rimmed glasses. Since he wasn't able to get home to California, he spent lots of time over the holidays at our house. My mother nearly swooned when he walked in. He and Lynn drank wine and listened to Janis Joplin records for hours. Janis screeched "Piece of My Heart" and "Me and Bobby McGee" until the Christmas tree shook, but my parents didn't seem to mind.

I was envious of Lynn, who was allowed to have her boyfriend in our home. Jack was made comfortable and coddled over. My mother fed him continuously and my father engaged in meaningful conversation with him. Everyone was happy except me, painfully missing my Michael, who seemed to be the family scourge. Why couldn't they see the good that I saw in him? And why did my mother have such a problem with me leaving the nest?

By design, my parents intentionally avoided mentioning Michael's name, I suppose to pretend that he didn't really exist. I was confused and frustrated that Mom seemed to like my engagement ring but despised the man who gave it to me. I was annoyed by her continual chatter about how wonderful it would be for me to get back to school and to my theater studies. She suggested I get involved in the college drama club to make some 'like-minded new friends.' She was determined to make me forget about my hometown boyfriend by making university life seem irresistible. She asked if I wanted new curtains for my dorm room in exaggerated tones of enthusiasm. Her constant effort to drive a wedge between Michael and me was a stabbing thorn in my side. I don't want to go back. Can't you see that? But my only words were, "No, Mom, the curtains are fine." Curtains were the last thing on my troubled mind. She knew that, I'm sure, but she was frantic in her efforts to keep Michael and me apart.

In January of 1969, I packed up my stuff in a depressed stupor to return to college. I was bothered by my mother's ebullient disposition and was sure it was because I was putting 125 miles between my boyfriend and me. How could she not know how heartsick I was? The back bumper of my sister's maroon Corvair was several inches closer to the pavement than usual for the trip. The little car was loaded down with books, records, our clean clothes, and a supply of snack foods for dorm life.

"I'd like Hostess chocolate cupcakes, Mom," I told my mother when she asked what I'd like to take back to school to snack on. She was so thoughtful and generous. She thought of everything. Then she brought home Hostess Twinkies instead, explaining that she decided they would be a better choice since they wouldn't be so messy and apt to melt.

"Sure, whatever," I mumbled. I didn't have the energy or desire to squabble with her about her control tactics anymore. Dad helped us on our way, in his quiet unpretentious manner, by changing the oil in the car and filling the gas tank.

Commit to the Lord whatever you do,
and your plans will succeed.
Proverbs 16:3

Chapter 15

Within the first week of returning to school two letters arrived from my mother, encouraging me again to make some new friends. She suggested going out to local pubs where the college kids hung out to meet new people. I read between the lines, go out looking for a college man to date. Forget the kid back here at home. Find someone who will be successful in the corporate world and make lots of money. I'm sure she also wanted me to put away my love of animals and country life to become a city dweller who danced and glittered on Broadway. After all, New York City was her city and her dream was to be a performer. Surely, that was good enough for me.

In the second letter, she actually mentioned Michael by name. The distance between us seemed to give her the nerve to actually acknowledge that he was indeed a part of my life. Her remark, intended as good advice was, "If you think you love him, being apart should make your relationship stronger. Let time and distance be the test of your love. If, when you are done with school, you and Michael still want to date, you will know it's real."

Infuriated, I crumpled the letter and threw it in the trash. Four years? How dare she suggest such a thing? I already knew our love was real. We wanted to get married. She knew that. Then I brushed my tears aside and retrieved the letter. I smoothed it out on my bed carefully and then ripped it over and over again until it was a pathetic pile of shrapnel. I brushed it into the trash basket, threw on my coat, and went out into the frigid night.

I walked against the cold wind, leaning into the icy gusts. With each step, I became more determined. I strode past Harrison Dining Hall and on through the campus. Every window in Gordon Hall was brightly lit. Cheery yellow light spilled out on the sidewalks like pools of laughter. I could hear voices singing and shouting even through the howl of the winter wind. I passed a few students, heads bent against the biting wind, mittened hands pressing heavy books to their chests. This was an academic setting where young people came to learn. I did not belong here. This was not what I wanted, at least not now. I was wasting time and money. The words my mother had written played repeatedly in my mind. I thought back to the night I'd first run away from home last summer. I knew from the first step back then, that I was going where Michael was. Psychological separation from my family of origin would be difficult because of the powerful guilt feeling I experienced, but I was ready. I walked until I was near exhaustion and my toes were numb, but I knew what I had to do. When I finally made my way back to my dorm, I knew undeniably, where I needed to start the journey to find myself.

I called Michael. "Come and get me," I stated simply, without even saying hello. It had only been a week since I had returned to school for the second semester.

"What?" he asked, bewildered.

"I can't do this anymore Michael," I sobbed, "please, can you come?" He offered some suggestions, but my mind was made up. "I am wasting my parents' money and my own money and time." I felt strong. "Please Michael. I can't stay here another day."

"OK, he finally offered, "Pack up your stuff. I'll ask for tomorrow off. I'll be there tonight." While I waited for his arrival, I telephoned my sister across campus and asked her to be my maid of honor at our wedding.

"Jeanne, I can't. Mom would kill me," was her response. I was hurt but I understood. That was the kind of control my mother had over her family.

Two hours later when the black Chevy pulled in, I was waiting in the stairwell on the ground floor. I pushed the heavy metal door open and jumped in the car before it came to a full stop.

Mike drew back from my tearful embrace and said flat out, "You can't stay in my parents' house with me." I nodded. We packed the car with all of my belongings. We drove off leaving Brockport for the last time. I wondered what was next.

> Each heart knows its own bitterness,
> and no one else can share its joy.
> Proverbs 14:10

Chapter 16

When we arrived in our hometown again, I had no idea where I would stay, how I would eat or sleep. How foolish and careless I was to assume someone would take care of me! It never occurred to Michael or me that living together without being married was an option. It was called 'shacking up,' and back in the day it was considered disgraceful and a total disregard for society's rules. Since Michael lived in his parents' house alone, it would have been convenient and easy for us to stay together there.

Thankfully, Mike was a sensible and take-charge person. I wondered if I had exchanged my mother's tenacious bossiness for Michael's caretaker personality. I was, after all, accustomed to the unhealthy position of having others take care of me and make decisions for me. By the end of my first day as a college drop out, he had arranged for a place for me to stay. Michael had left his job with the well-drilling company to work full time at the service station. He pumped gas and repaired vehicles.

Michael had confided in his boss, who owned the business. He explained the situation with my parents and us. His boss was a jovial fellow, not much older than Mike and me. His wife was a very gentle woman, they had two small children, and lived in a small house in Canastota. I was invited to stay with this family until Mike and I were married.

I felt self-conscious and uncomfortable when I arrived. The children eyed me suspiciously, but the boss's wife welcomed me warmly. She led me to their guest room, showed me how to operate the shower, and left clean towels for me. I tried my best to explain my courtship with Michael and my parents' disapproval. I apologized for barging in on her and her family, but she reassured me that I was safe and welcome. At bedtime, I quietly closed the door to the guest room, climbed into bed and slipped my thumb into my mouth.

Michael and I got busy preparing for our wedding. We made an appointment to speak with Father Behr, the priest at St Agatha's Church. He began pre-marital classes with us and we met at the church several times to learn about the sanctity of marriage and the rules of the Roman Catholic Church. Michael was raised Catholic, but did not attend mass. While I grew up in the Presbyterian Church, I hadn't attended in years either, so it didn't make much of a difference to us where we took our vows. We decided on a date, February 15th and Father Behr said the church would be free for a wedding ceremony that day. We had just three weeks to get ready.

We got the required blood tests. There was no time or money to make the 2-hour drive back to Sibley's to pick up the wedding gown that waited there for me. I forfeited my down payment and Mike took me shopping locally one evening for something to wear on our wedding day. He waited patiently in the car while I practically ran from store to store looking for a suitable dress. Just as the stores were closing, I decided on a street length white brocade dress with short sleeves. It was a plain A-line dress, which was a popular style at that time. I couldn't help but compare it to the velvet wedding dress that I would never wear, but it would have to do. I bought plain white shoes with a strap. They were the only pair I could find without a high heel. I didn't want to accentuate the fact that I was taller than Mike. I wanted to wear a veil of some kind and decided to make one to save money. I bought 2 yards of 1-inch white velvet ribbon and 2 yards of white netting, fashioned a large ribbon bow, and sewed it to a hair comb. Then I did the best I could with the netting. It was stiff and difficult to work with because I had purchased the nylon netting used to make pot scrubbers. I didn't know that soft, finely woven bridal veil material was available. On my wedding day, I looked like the Flying Nun, with a garish bow plopped on top of my head and a veil cut too short, that stuck out at odd angles around my face. Michael paid for the entire ensemble and for that I was very grateful. His parents took him shopping to buy a black suit, the first he had ever owned.

    I only spent a few weeks with the boss's family and tried to help as much as I could. I babysat the children and washed the dishes every night. "What else can I do?" I asked repeatedly, feeling indebted to them for their kindness and hospitality. I tried to give the family as much privacy as possible and spent most of my time in the guest room preparing for our wedding day.

    One day I was addressing wedding invitations when I heard a knock on the guest room door.

> Likewise, the tongue is a small part of the body, but it makes great boasts. Consider what a great forest is set on fire by a small spark.
> James 3:5

Chapter 17

"Jeanne, your mother just pulled in," was the muffled message from the other side of the door. Somehow, my parents found out I had left school and was back in town. I surmised that a friend had probably told them and vowed not to share any more personal information with my friends away at college.

My mother, indignant and bold, knocked on the front door. My heart pounded in my ears as I headed toward the insistent rapping at the front door. The all too familiar feeling of dread enveloped me as I opened the door and stepped out on the porch. "I want you to come home with me right now!" she snapped. "What do you think you are doing, living with these people? Don't you have any sense?"

I ignored her remarks and tried to use my gentlest voice, "Mom, Michael and I are getting married at St. Agatha's on February 15th. Mom, please, please won't you come? I want you and Daddy to be there. I want your blessing." I wanted her to be as excited as I was.

She seemed to be listening to me so, energized, I ran to get the engraved wedding invitations I had been working on. "Look, Mom." She stared at me for a few seconds, without looking at the invitations in my hand. Then she sucked in cigarette smoke as if it was pure oxygen and exploded. She shook and trembled as she called Michael every name she could think of. She stepped closer to me and thrust a finger in my face. I did not move.

"You are NOT going to marry that boy and I will see to it that you don't. I will stop this wedding if it's the last thing I do. Mark my words."

Fury rose in me and I egged her on, "Oh yes I am," I replied self-righteously, crossing my arms.

"Don't toy with me, Jeanne," she said evenly, her words barbed.

I lost my temper and shouted, "I am marrying Michael, and there is nothing you can do about it. I am asking you to give us your blessing. If you won't, then fine. I can't believe you're doing this to me!" It didn't occur to me to consider what she might be experiencing as a mother. Rivers of tears trickled down my cheeks and dripped off my chin but I refused to wipe them away. I resisted the overwhelming urge to slam the door in her face.

"You just wait." she sneered in staccato for emphasis. She spun around on her heels and huffed toward her car.

I followed her, feeling panic rising in my throat, "Mom, please. Please!" I begged, as she slammed her car door and sped away.

The boss's wife crept out of the kitchen. "Are you OK?" she asked.

I nodded and cried, "I am so sorry. See what I mean about her?"

I returned to the guest room where our wedding invitations lay scattered and in disarray. I was frightened by my own rage. I felt such loathing and frustration for my mother at that point. I mulled over the terrible exchange that had just taken place. Her words of warning pounded in my ears. "Just you wait. I will stop this wedding if it's the last thing I do." Then panic overwhelmed me, like a tornado spinning and destroying everything in its path.

That evening I relayed all the awful details about my conversation with my mother to Michael. Now we were both afraid that she would show up at the church and ruin our wedding day. We talked about how to handle the new threat that my mother might actually try to stop our wedding. Would she walk into the church and object publicly, ruining our ceremony? Would she try physically dragging me out of the church? My imagination went wild with possibilities. We talked to Father Behr and secretly moved the wedding date up two weeks. If we could keep the new date from my parents, we would be married before they knew it. With the priest's approval, we changed the date to February 1st. Because we had so little money, we could not afford to have new invitations printed, so I carefully drew a line through February 15, 1969 and penned February 1, 1969 in my best handwriting. And that's how the few invitations went out. There was no other way.

> For this reason a man will leave his father and mother
> and be united to his wife,
> and the two will become one flesh.
> Ephesians 5:31

Chapter 18

As quickly as a bride can throw her bouquet, our wedding was upon us. We did what we could to make it a meaningful and joyous occasion on our meager budget. There were no flowers decorating the church, no elaborate unity candles, photographer, or special music. Since Michael's boss and his wife had been so kind to us in the weeks preceding our wedding, we asked them to sign our marriage license as witnesses.

There was no snow falling on the day we were married, but February 1st was a bitter cold day, so frigid that the snow squeaked and protested under one's shoes.

There was no sun and the icicles hung along St Agatha's church like stalactites.

My hosts drove me to the church. Right away I noticed Michael's car in the parking lot along with several others. I felt my heart jump and thought to myself, he is here to become my husband. It was a thrilling notion. I tiptoed through the ice and into the church and was met by Father Behr. His bald head seemed to be especially shiny and reflected the lights overhead. He smiled broadly. "Are you ready, Jeanne?" he asked, holding my hand. I nodded. He went over last minute details and moved to the front of the church. Michael had a boutonniere and small bouquet of roses delivered to the church. The flowers were perfect for the dress I wore. Tiny white sweetheart roses and baby breath were drawn together in a lacy cone with satin ribbon.

I stood in the vestibule alone, watching the street for signs of my mother and father. Then I remembered that surely they didn't know that today was the day I was marrying Michael. But deep in my heart I held on to the hope that somehow, perhaps they would come to be a part of this special day. Did my parents think they were acting appropriately by not participating in our wedding? My mother was angry with me for growing up and away from her, and Dad supported her position. It would take years to work through the feelings of guilt I experienced for disobeying them.

Suddenly I heard the priest's voice welcoming our guests. That was my cue to ready myself for the walk, alone, down the center aisle. I thought of my dad and how handsome he would look if he were here to walk me down the aisle today. I sighed sadly. Then I turned my back to the windows that faced the icy street outside.

The sanctuary was warm and bathed in lovely golden light. Only three people sat on the bride's side of the church, a trio of my friends who had made the trip home from college. No one from my family was at the church. My mother made sure of that. Most of my friends were away at school. On my right, scattered in the pews sat two dozen of Michael's friends and family. My groom, in a brand new black suit and tie, stood with Father Behr at the front of the church. Michael's smile beckoned me from afar to move forward. With my eyes fastened on him, I made my way, alone, to the altar.

As long as I did not look away from Michael's handsome face, I was not nervous. He was my grounding rod and my rock. We took our vows and, for the moment, forgot all the trouble and roadblocks we had encountered to get to this place. We were surprised and pleased when the church organist played and an altar boy sang during the ceremony. Father Behr must have arranged for the music for the ceremony, free of charge.

Focused solely on each other, we promised before God and man that we would love and cherish each other until our deaths. I knew I was doing the right thing and spoke with conviction. I did not know that as I said, "I do," my father was pulling away from the curb on a side street near the church. Alone, he had watched me as I entered St. Agatha's in my white dress on that white winter day.

After the ceremony, we had a small party at the tavern that Mike's parents owned. His mother made sure we had a wedding cake and she prepared lots of food for the guests. His dad stood behind the bar and kept everyone's drinks full. Michael and Harry entertained the crowd with their guitar picking and song. As I watched Michael's nimble fingers on the guitar strings and heard his mellow voice, I felt so proud that he was my husband. I was overwhelmed that, after dating Mike for a year and a half, my desire was finally fulfilled. I knew my destiny was to share my life with this man.

I felt a sense of closure in my heart. I knew I was saying goodbye to my identity as a moody, cranky, and disobedient teen. Ahead lay the responsibilities of an adult and all that came with it. I was happy to walk through that new portal and charge ahead with my life because I had Michael beside me. I thanked God that He gave me the wisdom to recognize an unhealthy situation and the strength to step toward independence. On that bittersweet wedding day, without my parents' blessing, I cried and laughed, sometimes simultaneously.

The party after the wedding was fun and noisy. The people that had gathered to celebrate with us seemed genuinely happy for us. Harry's dad whispered with a devilish grin, "Mike, call me if you get into any trouble," and he pressed a ten dollar bill into my new husband's hand.

We ate good food and cut our wedding cake. I threw my little bouquet over my shoulder and Michael and I scampered out into the night, together at last.

Jeanne Wilhite Dunn

A wife of noble character is her husband's crown,
but a disgraceful wife is like decay in his bones.
Proverbs 12:4

Chapter 19

We are on our way to Tennessee. Chelsea, our oldest granddaughter is graduating from high school in Knoxville. She made it look easy to change schools at the beginning of her senior year. She was raised in California and left her lifelong friends and her school to move to Tennessee with her family. Her graduation is as much of a milestone for us as it is for Chelsea.

Michael has the cruise control on and we are fast approaching a white Acura moving slower than us. Michael switches to the passing lane and as we pass, I notice a 'Just Married' sign in the back window.

"Michael, newlyweds!"

He honks the horn and we wave wildly. Smiling, the young couple wave back and toot in reply. We are enthusiastic supporters of marriage.

"I bet they're on their honeymoon," I offer wistfully. My husband reaches for my hand and squeezes it. I slip into a reverie where I find myself back in Niagara Falls, the honeymoon capital of the world, for the very first time.

*****

The frigid air of February had stilled the roaring waters, but Niagara Falls sparkled with rainbow hues. The Niagara River was silent and still now that it was February and heavy ice hung over the falls suffocating the rocks underneath. As we stood hand-in-hand at the iron railing, Michael and I were sure the incredible light display had been created just for us. The mighty river had nearly stopped its eternal churning, at least on the surface.

We were sure that the torment of teen years and our anxiety would cease now that we were married. We were rich and happy honeymooners. Mike's wallet was fat with the $217.00 he had saved up for this trip. Our clothes lay, neatly folded in brown paper sacks in the back seat of the car. Harry and Gladys had written 'Just Married' with white shoe polish in the back window.

Finally, it was all right for us to be alone, sleep and eat together, talk and to dream as a couple.

Our first night as husband and wife was a confusing concoction of fatigue, fear, relief, and regret. Somehow, despite the monumental adversity we faced, we had done it. We were elated that we officially belonged to one another. Somehow, I got through a terribly painful day with him by my side. As happy as I was, I cried every night while we were away, overcome with guilt and shame for disobeying my parents. Michael held me in his arms at night while I whimpered, unable to give voice to my anguish and confusion. He waited patiently until I stopped and then looked deep into my eyes and murmured, "You OK now?" I snuggled into his chest and nodded. Nevertheless, fear plagued me even as I dreamed. Had my parents forsaken me forever? Would I ever see my sister and brothers again? Was it wrong for me to love Michael so much? I lay awake until I heard my new husband's breathing become slow and deep with sleep. Only then, did I turn away, rub the blanket gently on my nose, and suck my thumb until I too, slept.

The following day we crossed the border into Canada and at 18 years old, I was excited to be outside the United States for the first time. I was confident that Mike would take care of me and rather disappointed when the foreign land looked just like home. During the day, it was easy to pretend all was well. I smiled and tried to act as I thought a newlywed should. We tramped through the slushy streets to Louis Tussauds Wax Museum and to see all the amazing things on display in Ripley's Believe It or Not Museum. But I was filled with thoughts of how I had hurt my parents and the sights and sounds were only a momentary distraction for me.

We took the elevator to the top of the Skylon Tower Restaurant. We stepped into the revolving restaurant and had dinner. As the restaurant slowly turned, we peeked at the beautiful night sky from over 700 feet in the air. I looked out and felt somehow close to heaven, and offered up a silent prayer that God would forgive me for all the heartache I caused back home. Lost in the beautiful view and my thoughts, Michael softly touched my elbow, "You OK?" he asked lovingly for the hundredth time.

We found the stairwell and took the stairs down 52 stories to the ground level. I felt like a carefree child, out of breath and laughing all the way down. Alone in the echoing stairwell with my new husband I shouted, "I love you, Michael Dunn!" We were young and silly, but we had done what we knew was right for us. I felt I was ready to be a wife and helpmate. Our money had dwindled down to $17.00 but love and devotion were in plentiful supply. Together we could overcome anything life handed us. We packed up our belongings and a handful of tiny black and white pictures taken in Niagara Falls with a borrowed Polaroid camera. It was time to go home.

Jeanne Wilhite Dunn

Trust in the Lord with all your heart and lean not on your own understanding, in all your ways acknowledge him and he will make your paths straight.
Proverbs 3:5-6

Chapter 20

We returned from our honeymoon to Canastota to find that the service station where Mike worked had gone out of business. Michael had lost his only means of income and we knew the $17.00 left in his wallet would not last long. We found jobs and a small apartment within the first week. I found a job at Cerio's Modern Market working in the meat and deli department. They offered to pay $1.60 per hour, the minimum wage. I was happy with that, considering I was unskilled labor and needed on-the-job training. I learned every cut of meat and how to label and wrap it. Before long, I knew the name of every salami and cheese that they offered. It was a small family-run business right in our hometown and they seemed happy to offer a job to a local girl like me.

Michael was hired as a full time factory worker at Oneida Limited Silversmith Factory, making the handles for silverware knives. It was a tedious and dangerous job. He operated a drop hammer that stamped the design in the knife handles and the machine would take a finger clean off if the operator was distracted even for a moment. It was a noisy, dirty job and Michael came home smelling like solvent. I loved him even more when he was dirty and smelled funny. I knew I had married a man who was diligent and hard working. I knew he would be a good provider.

We found a tiny upstairs apartment located out in the country on a back road that I had never heard of. Thank goodness, it was furnished since we had no furniture and very few belongings. We spent that spring and summer in the apartment that we would eventually come to detest. The ceilings slanted this way and that and plastic curtains hung in the tiny dirty windows. The living room had one big throne-like chair with flat wooden arms, a wobbly end table, and a black and white TV. The television was an enormous thing, roughly the size of a large washing machine with two metal antenna protruding out of the top, 'rabbit ears,' that we wiggled this way and that to get a picture on the screen. We spent frustrating hours trying to determine what we were looking at on the snowy television screen.

One hot July evening we turned on the TV and frantically wiggled the rabbit ear antenna. "What's that?" Michael asked.

"I can't really tell," I replied, staring through the snow and lines on the screen, "I think it's Neil Armstrong!"

Then we heard a crackling voice through the static, "That's one small step for man, one giant leap for mankind." We had missed the images of the first man to walk on the moon. It was July 20, 1969.

When we were both in the bed that dominated the small bedroom, we had to hold on to the edge of the mattress to keep from rolling on top of each other in the big hollow in the middle. Flipping the mattress did no good. It was the bare metal springs under the mattress that were worn out and sagging. We laughed happily when we met in the middle and our young vertebrae never seemed to object to the lack of support. I was not accustomed to such repulsive furnishings, but I would have lived in a cardboard box just to be with Michael.

One night as we lay in bed talking, I began to describe to Michael the circumstances surrounding my parents' marriage. "Michael, they only knew each other for 60 days before they married," I said. "The only people there were Mom's best friend, Alyce, and some friend of my father's from his ship. After they got married, my father had to go back to his ship and my mother went to live with her aunt in Queens."

"Where is that?' asked Mike.

"It's part of New York City. Anyway, my mother was only 17 when she married Dad and he was 21," I continued. "Of course Dad's parents were long gone, but my mother's parents weren't at her wedding either."

We could not help but compare the two relationships. My parents only knew each other for 60 days before getting married. Mike and I dated a year and a half. On our wedding days, Mom was only 17 years old and I was 18, almost 19 years old. My mother's parents were not supportive of her hasty decision to marry my father, nor were they present at her wedding. So why had they made the passage to matrimony so difficult for Michael and me? Didn't they remember the hurt and pain of parental opposition?

"I have to believe they really thought they were acting appropriately and in our best interest, Michael." I said.

"Well, they weren't," he concluded.

"I know." Now that I had gotten what I wanted, to be Michael's wife, I regretted the cruel things I had said and done earlier. I could not understand how loving

Michael granted me such happiness, and caused my parents such heartache. It simply didn't make sense.

I tried to cook in our little apartment, but with only one saucepan, two dishes and a pair of forks and spoons (taken from Harrison Dining Hall) it was not an easy task. I served Michael lots of canned soup and macaroni and cheese from a box. He seemed happy and ate heartily. I didn't have much of an appetite. The smell of my own cooking made me queasy.

After only a few months, we suspected that the property owner, who lived downstairs, was coming into our apartment frequently when we were away. We became stealthy detectives and came up with a clandestine plan. We sprinkled powder on the floors one day just before we left, and carefully backed out the door.

Sure enough, later that day we returned to discover footprints in every room of the apartment. Michael was livid. He immediately went downstairs and gave notice that we would be moving within the next few weeks. Heated words volleyed back and forth and the property owner insisted he had every right to invade our privacy. Suddenly our little apartment appeared as it really was, nothing but a seedy, stale attic, with an ogre living underneath.

Jeanne Wilhite Dunn

> Anxiety weighs a person's heart down,
> but a kind word cheers him up.
> Proverbs 12:25

Chapter 21

I was slicing Genoa salami for a customer when I looked up to see my mother standing at the deli counter at the Modern Market. I looked down at the electric meat slicer I was using and continued to catch the slices and stack them neatly. As I wrapped the cold cuts in white butcher paper and tied the package with string, my heart thumped wildly in my chest. I croaked out a "thank you and have a good day" to the customer. I glanced at my mother. I was struck with how pleasantly familiar her face was, even though it had been months since I had seen her. Her expression was gentle and I could see affection for me in her eyes. It appeared that she had come to the realization that she was not going to be a part of my life because of the ultimatum she had made just before our wedding.

Evidently, she had changed her strategy and, I hoped, her heart. "Jeanne, there is a very nice apartment for rent on Main Street in the village," she began. "I will show you and Mike where it is and you can look at it. I hate to see you out there in the middle of nowhere in that tiny place." I wondered how she knew where we lived, but I didn't ask. This seemed to be a peace offering of sorts.

I talked to Mike. He was cautious, but the fact that she was concerned about us and seemed interested in our lives made us hopeful. We looked at and loved the duplex Mom had discovered. It had big rooms downstairs, two bedrooms upstairs and was spotless. The couple who owned the house, Norman and Lillian, lived on the other side. They were good-natured and friendly. It seemed perfect. On moving day, my parents presented us with a late 'wedding gift' as they called it. A brand new full size bed with mattress and box springs arrived at our new address, 217 North Main Street. Mike and I looked at each other in disbelief and began to giggle with the irony of it. I blushed with embarrassment that my parents would give us something that, to me, represented the most intimate aspect of our relationship. Actually, I think they just wanted us to have a comfortable place to lay our heads and sleep.

By now it was well into summer and life was good. It was an especially hot summer and the heat seemed to make me nauseous and give me headaches. We splurged and bought a fan for our apartment and I sipped ginger ale and tried to keep cool. My parents were speaking to us again and seemed to be accepting our marriage. Although the conversation was strained at times, we did talk. Mom brought some household essential for us each time she visited, a lamp, some kitchen utensils, potholders, towels. I felt like I was in paradise. We had a beautiful apartment, we were both earning money, and our family loved us.

Then an official-looking letter arrived from the government in our mailbox. It was a notice from the draft board ordering Michael to present himself for a military physical exam. When I told my mother she shook her head disgustedly and said, "Well that's just great. How are you going to get along when you're all alone? Maybe you should have thought things out better." I hoped she would have been more sympathetic, but apparently, she saw it as an 'I told you so' moment.

We were relieved and surprised when Michael did not pass the draft physical. Although he appeared fit and healthy, he had stomach ulcers. The army doctors verified that he had them since he was a small child and they felt he was too great a medical risk to join the armed forces. The vast majority of young men were being sent to the war in Vietnam. Although Michael felt badly that he would never serve his country overseas, we were grateful he was out of harm's way. After that little bump in the road, we were even more appreciative of each other.

We had one car and Michael needed it to get to work in Sherrill, which was 10 miles away, but I walked the two blocks to work at the Modern Market. I also enjoyed walking to the bank, the library and my parents' house. I felt there was a healing occurring in my relationship with my mother. Nothing was mentioned about the terrible things we had said to one another in the past. But the air was still pregnant with the possibility of one of us saying something that would spark a quarrel.

One blistering, hot day the mercury rocketed over the 90 mark on the thermometer outside our kitchen window. Dressed in shorts and a cool top, I set out to walk several blocks to the post office. I bought a stamp, mailed a letter to a friend in college, and turned to leave. I looked up at the familiar mural over the doors of the post office of Canastota's onion farmers at work on the mucklands. For as long as I could remember, I never left the post office without admiring the beautiful historic painting. But that day I felt a wave of queasiness and the world went black and silent. I had fainted and slipped to the marble floor in the post office lobby.

Jeanne Wilhite Dunn

Not only so, but we also rejoice in our sufferings,
because we know that suffering
produces perseverance.
Romans 5:3

Chapter 22

I was embarrassed but unharmed in the post office incident, and a trip to the doctor confirmed the good news. I was expecting! Michael and I were both elated to discover that our first baby was on the way. According to the doctor, the baby was due on March 15, 1970. Physically, I was not handling my pregnancy very well. I became so sick and dehydrated from continuous vomiting that I was hospitalized for 13 days. "Shut the door please," I asked each nurse as she left my hospital room. It was the only way I could suck my thumb. I was medicated, rehydrated with IV fluids, discharged and then went home only to continue vomiting everything I ate. Even a sip of water or a cracker would trigger uncontrolled vomiting.

My mother was very concerned about my condition and she offered all kinds of suggestions. Once again she began calling me "Babe." She always used this loving nickname when I was sick as a child. I enjoyed hearing it again and it brought back fond memories and feelings of love and security. She was such a good mom when I was sick. She brought home ginger ale, as a remedy and special treat when I complained of a tummy ache. She was a proponent of Vicks Vapo-Rub, Mercurochrome and cold washcloths. I ran to the bathroom for what seemed like the hundredth time that day. I heard a whispered conversation between retching. "Michael, you have to do something about her being so sick."

Irritated, Mike shot back, "We are doing everything the doctor said to do. What more do you want?"

Exasperated, she left, only to call me a short time later. "Let me call the doctor," she said. I warned her not to do so. We were very capable of taking care of ourselves and contacting the doctor when needed. But Mom's concern finally got the best of her and caused her to, once again, overstep her boundaries. I knew she loved me fiercely. Never have I doubted my mother's love for me. In fact, I realize now that it was her love for me that was the driving force behind her interactions with me. Even when she made poor parenting decisions, I knew she loved me. And I loved her.

She telephoned Michael late the following afternoon to see how I was getting along. Again, she insisted that Michael do something about my constant nausea. I was so miserable and guilt-ridden that I was the cause of escalating friction again. When Mom felt she wasn't getting any satisfaction with Mike she blurted out, "Well, the doctor called *me* this morning." Anger welled up in Michael. Not only was he angry with her, but even more so with the doctor for sharing what should have been confidential medical information. A loud fight ensued. He slammed the phone down, immediately drove to the doctor's office, and demanded to speak with him.

When Michael began his frustrated rant, the doctor held up his hand and interrupted "Whoa! Whoa, Mr. Dunn. Your mother-in-law called *me*! I was just returning the call! I had no idea what she wanted. And I did not share any of your wife's medical information with her."

This was just another way Mom could manipulate. She was truthful when she said the doctor had called her, although she conveniently left out some important details. She was trying to make us believe that the doctor placed more importance on her than on my husband. A part of me understood her concern. She was trying to let go and allow me to be an adult, albeit a young adult, but her empathy and mother's concern for my health got the best of her.

And we know that in all things God works
for the good of those who love him,
who have been called according to his purpose.
Romans 8:28

Chapter 23

Eric calls from his cell phone. "Hey!" he says, his trademark greeting every time he calls home. He lives in Tennessee now.

"Hi there Eric! What's up?" I am always happy to hear his voice.

"Nothing really. I'm on my way to the lumber store. Remember that deck project I told you about? I should be finishing it up this week. The customer is real

happy with my work." Eric is a general contractor, a good one. I think he gets his talent from his dad.

"Eric, your birthday is coming up soon. Is there something special you'd...."

My son cuts me off. "Mom, I gotta go. I just stopped for a mocha at the drive-thru and I don't have enough hands." *He's always so busy, just like his dad.*

"OK, love you, Eric." And he is gone. Hearing his voice brings to mind the day of his birth. I can hardly believe it was 45 years ago.

*****

Eric Gabriel Dunn was born on St Patrick's Day of 1970. Fathers were strictly forbidden in the delivery room. I gave birth to Michael's son while he paced in the waiting room. When the nurses wheeled me from the labor room to delivery, I begged them to let Michael come with me, to no avail. We had made it clear that we did not want either my parents or Michael's parents present until after the baby was born. I knew it hurt my mother that we had been firm in excluding her from this important event, but we were fearful she might become so anxious that she would interfere. We assured both families that we would call for them to join us at the hospital after the baby's birth. We wanted to experience the birth of our first baby alone.

The day of Eric's birth was the happiest day of our lives. When the hospital staff finally let my husband join me in the recovery room, we held each other close and soaked each other with tears of joy and relief. Somehow, this wailing seven pound human being had arrived on the scene and reinforced our bond to each other. Our new role as parents brought us even closer together and Eric was the adhesive agent. This tiny person, in diapers and an undershirt, represented our love, in a tangible way. It was a poignant moment the first time Michael tenderly held his son. He was completely at ease with the baby. Eric was a part of me, a part of Michael, and a new entity that sealed our love for each other forever. After Michael and I held, and bonded with our new baby, family began to stream into my hospital room.

Eric was the first grandchild of both the Dunns and the Wilhites. Mike's father especially, was so proud the day of his grandson's birth. He was of Irish heritage and a baby boy born on St. Patrick's Day was a cause for serious celebrating. There was liquor and bragging at his workplace that day. I made sure Mom was the first person to hold the baby. Witnessing the obvious love she had for Baby Eric, I was sure my mother would now grow to love and respect my husband. After all, Michael and I had given her the extraordinary gift of her very first grandchild. We brought our baby home, to our Main Street apartment, knowing our lives would be richer.

The new grandmothers took turns holding Eric and tried to decide who he resembled. My heart melted to see them side by side, engrossed in the baby, putting differences aside. Jamie and Mikey were now youthful little uncles at 6 and 4 years old. Mikey was so excited to meet Eric that he showed up with a clip-on bowtie attached to his turtleneck shirt. "He dressed himself for the occasion," Mom said, with a twinkle in her eye. My sister, Lynn, now married and expecting her own baby in July, got in some practice changing diapers. Eric was happy to oblige. It seemed that his arrival brought peace and harmony to an unpredictable family.

With so many family members and friends in and out of our apartment, Mom tried hard to treat Michael and me as adults and not brainless idiots. Nevertheless, wanting her little grandson to thrive, she couldn't help but ask, "Jeanne, are you sure you're boiling his bottles long enough to sterilize them?"

"Yes, Mom."

"You're using Dreft soap to wash his diapers, right?

"Yes, Mom."

"You know not to use bleach, don't you?"

"Yes, Mom."

I knew she was feeling a bit out of control and wanted the best for her grandbaby. After all, it was only a few years before that she had babies of her own in the house. She knew the drill. Mike and I were patient and appreciated her input.

Later, when Eric was a toddler and feverish, she was always the first person I called for advice. My new role as a mother seemed to help me to mature and realize that my parents were not out to ruin my life, as I had thought just a few years back. They had good advice to offer and wanted the best for my family and me. So our sweet baby boy grew, knowing and loving all four of his grandparents.

Motherhood was an absolute delight for me. I had a very strong maternal instinct and found tremendous satisfaction in nurturing and caring for Eric. I spent hours rocking our baby boy and gazing down at him. I caressed his perfect little ears and kissed his eyebrows. I was overwhelmed with love for him. His Daddy loved to hold and cuddle Eric and was perfectly comfortable with his baby boy in his arms right from the start.

Jeanne Wilhite Dunn

> By wisdom a house is built,
> and through understanding it is established;
> through knowledge its rooms are filled
> with rare and beautiful treasures.
> Proverbs 24:3-4

Chapter 24

Mike grumbles to himself all the way back to the house from the mailbox. He opens the tax bills and gripes about the amount due. We have 45 acres of croplands, pasture, and woodlands. "Must be the taxes are so high because we own the building lot next door," I offer.

He growls, throws the bills aside, and pats my behind. "All that money, just to keep you happy here on the farm," he snickers. Frog Hollow Homestead has grown over the years and so have the taxes. We added a big sunroom to the back of the house and built a freestanding garage for Mike's motorcycles and his antique car. In addition to the main barn, we now have a freestanding chicken coop, a barn for the goats and three ponds. I think back to the little parcel of land with which we started our homestead.

*****

As much as we enjoyed Norm and Lillian's apartment on Main Street, we longed for a home of our own. The summer following Eric's birth, we began taking drives around the countryside looking for a parcel of land to buy. By now we had been married for a year and a half and had decided we would build our own house. Several times I had watched as Michael tramped out into open fields and barnyards, looking for land owners who might have a parcel to sell. It never occurred to us to contact a realtor to buy land. Young and inexperienced, we thought if you wanted to buy land, you just went to the person who owned some and asked.

On a warm June afternoon, we stopped on the side of North Court Street and Mike got out of our blue Volkswagen bug. Eric sat on my lap and gurgled. I smiled down at him and shooed a fly out of the car through the open window. I watched Michael stumble out into the freshly plowed land toward a groaning red tractor in the middle of the field. Mike approached the farmer, Weston Hilts, who climbed down from his Farmall. As Mike spoke, Mr. Hilts looked down, dug the toe of his boot into the freshly turned sod, and nodded thoughtfully. Michael spoke for a long time. The farmer looked up and gestured to the north and south. I strained to hear what he was saying, but all I could hear were the summer birds singing and a fly buzzing angrily around the perimeter of the windshield. I watched as they shook hands and Mike turned to make his way back to the car. Mr. Hilts stood and watched him for a long time before climbing back up on his tractor.

My husband got back in the car and threw his head back until it bumped on the back of the drivers' seat. He closed his eyes and sighed. "What?" I said anxiously.

He rolled his head toward Eric and me, "We just bought us some land!" he replied, with a wide grin. Mr. Hilts had agreed to sell us 9/10 of an acre of land adjacent to the very land he was plowing! Michael had explained that we had $720 to spend and the price of this odd-shaped parcel of land was, according to Mr. Hilts, exactly $700.

We liked the area, which was flat, had good roads, nice homes, and was halfway between Canastota and Oneida. We did not realize how swampy it was, but we were proud landowners at the age of 20. I lifted the baby up in celebration until his back brushed the headliner in the VW. "Woo Hoo, Eric! Your Daddy did good!" I rejoiced. Eric responded by spitting up curdled milk in my lap. Mike and I laughed until our sides ached.

Our bank account was empty, but we felt sure we had made a good investment. We bought a second-hand lawnmower and once our parcel of land was surveyed and deeded to us, we mowed the weeds down and began picking up rocks. Several times during that year, we drove to Court Street, spread an old quilt out in the bristly grass, laid Eric in the middle and ate a picnic dinner together. Eric kicked his feet and made baby sounds at the clouds. We talked about building our house. I began checking out Better Homes and Gardens magazines from the library. Each magazine featured a different floor plan with blueprints available for purchase. I poured over the floor plans and tried to imagine what each room might look like.

"Look at this one, Mike. It has an entryway with a skylight!" I said, handing him the magazine. He looked at me and closed the magazine.

"Honey," he said, "I hate to tell you this, but I don't know how to read blueprints," he confessed. Not to be discouraged, we brought out some notebook paper and pencils. We decided on the total length and width of the house and plotted out where we wanted each room.

In the meantime, God was blessing us abundantly. On a whim, Michael answered a US Postal Service employment ad that he found on a piece of junk mail. Amazingly, the post office contacted him for an interview. He took the civil service test, passed, and was hired part-time as a letter carrier. We knew the postal service paid well, offered great benefits, and had an outstanding retirement system. He liked being outdoors all day and made many friends along his route. We waited almost two years until a full-time permanent position became available. When it did, Michael got the position.

Mike worked on our land whenever he had the opportunity. He put in a septic tank and leach field and called Ernie, a former co-worker, to drill a well on the property. Warm days and money quickly became in short supply, so progress came to a standstill for the winter. We still had a cozy home in our apartment on Main Street. The three of us stayed tucked in while the snow drifted by the big windows that faced the street light in front. We dreamed of North Court Street and the house that would materialize there soon. We saved every penny we could through the winter months.

By spring of 1971, we had enough money saved to purchase a used 10 X 50 foot mobile home. We moved it on to our land. We would live there until the house was finished. We no longer had to pay rent each month, so our money went for building materials. We paid cash for everything and bought supplies a little at a time. We never had a house mortgage.

Our $1800 temporary trailer home was old, but we fixed it up as much as money would allow. We painted Eric's bedroom walls bright yellow and painted the built-in dresser drawers orange. I bought fabric printed with ducklings dancing in the grass and sewed curtains to flutter at the windows.

The living room walls were bare, so I cut photos from old magazines and made a collage on a big piece of cardboard. Michael hung it over the ragged sofa. We had acquired a small record player and a few records, including an album by Simon and Garfunkel. I played it over and over while I cleaned, cooked and cared for our beautiful baby. I was profoundly happy. When I dressed Eric each morning after his bath in the bathroom sink, I smiled down at his baby face and sang "Bridge Over Troubled Water." As I sang the lyrics, I promised Eric I would dry all his tears for the rest of his life. Hearing that song would forever remind me of Eric and those wonderful early days so full of anticipation and joy.

As Eric grew to be a toddler, I was sure we had the smartest and most beautiful child in the world. Eric and I sat in the hallway for hours where I taped the letters of the alphabet, pictures of animals, people, and places, all at his eye level. We talked about everything and I loved teaching our son new things every day. Nothing else seemed important when I felt Eric's familiar weight on my lap and his head on my chest as we read books together.

Somehow, miraculously, Michael was able to build our four-bedroom Cape Cod style house according to the crude drawing we made on that lined notebook paper. In the next several years, we also built a barn, dug a pond, and bought more land adjacent to the parcel we owned. Our focus was on establishing our farm, which we named, "Frog Hollow Homestead." We thought the name appropriate after a myriad of toads and frogs in the swamp behind our house serenaded us each evening in the warm weather.

Our lives seemed to be idyllic, like the peaceful pond we had dug behind the house, but trouble churned just below the surface. I continued to suck my thumb, sometimes excessively, but somehow I was able to hide my bizarre vice from everyone. My mother continued her attempts to dominate me, but with exquisite delicacy. While Michael was supportive and patient with me, he would not tolerate any of my mother's attempts to control our lives. My mother seemed unable to stop her calculated maneuvers to subtly criticize. At least that's the way I saw it. Although I had been married over two years and was a mother, I still wanted to please my mother and father. I just couldn't figure out how to do that. I was learning the hard lesson that every time I gave undue power to my family of origin, I was compromising my marriage.

They seemed to love my sister's husband. He and Lynn had moved to Florida and had two beautiful little girls. They came to visit our parents every year. My parents, brothers and Lynn and her family went camping and hiking when they were together. I was hurt that I was the only sibling left out, but everyone knew that if Mike wasn't welcome, and usually he wasn't, I wasn't going anywhere without him. Besides we were busy living the country life right there on our little farm. Who needed to go camping to enjoy life?

> Children are a heritage from the Lord,
> children a reward from him.
> Psalm 127:3

Chapter 25

Our baby girl, Rebecca Lee, was born three years after Eric. Both Mike and I were sure all through the pregnancy that we would have another boy. In our minds, a family with an older boy and then a daughter was the epitome of perfection. With the ongoing friction with my parents, perhaps we felt we didn't deserve that. But when the doctor announced, "It's a little girl," in the delivery room, I felt like heaven had poured out its most precious treasure to us. I just couldn't believe I was the mother of a daughter. If our family was a package, Becki was the pink bow on top. God was granting me the privilege and chance to be the mother of a future bride. That day, I prayed that God would help me not to make the same mistakes my mom had made.

With my love of animals and nature, I never considered myself a particularly feminine person. I rarely wore make-up. Jeans and a T-shirt were my preference for clothing. I wondered if I would be able to raise a little girl. I considered ballet lessons, makeup, menstruation, dating, and her wedding all in the few moments it took the nurse to dry and swaddle our baby girl in the delivery room. I held out my arms eagerly to hold our daughter for the first time. She crumpled up her tiny pink face against the glare of the world and my heart just melted. "Will you let me tell my husband it's a girl?" I asked. The nurse's eyes sparkled over her white mask. She nodded and opened the heavy delivery room door just a crack.

"Michael?" I shouted.

"Yea, I'm here," he called back.

"It's a girl! We have a baby girl!" I cried as my voice broke. The nurse took Rebecca and I put my hands over my face and sobbed uncontrollably, feeling unworthy and blessed with this most perfect gift from God. My words had stunned Michael into silence. The nurse quietly closed the door.

At night when Rebecca's cry woke me for her 2 am feeding, I rocked her gently and dreamed of what she might become. Alone in the darkness with our precious newborn baby girl, I put my thumb in my mouth and rubbed Becki's baby blanket on my nose. I thought of how utterly outrageous the scene would look if I were caught. I had tried and tried to break this deplorable habit, but I was unable to stop. I was too humiliated to confide in anyone, including my husband, so I bore the unspeakable despair and hopelessness alone.

I braced myself subconsciously for a constant stream of suggestions regarding child rearing, but surprisingly, my mother did not criticize our parenting skills. She and Dad loved to spend time with both of our children. When Rebecca was born, Mom and Dad often took 3-year-old Eric for the afternoon to afford me some much-needed rest. As Becki grew, Gram loved having her granddaughter visit, and they grew to be very close. Together they shared secrets and explored Mom's attic and closets for special treasures. I was so thankful that Rebecca had such a special bond with her grandmother.

As we all do, Michael and I vowed we would avoid the mistakes our parents had made with us. We prayed daily for wisdom to raise our children in an emotionally healthy way. I was scared to death my daughter would turn out like me. We vowed to raise kids who would one day become independent. We would rejoice when they left the nest, and never make them feel guilty for growing up. We would not proliferate the unhealthy way of life that we experienced growing up.

Now we were four and our family was complete. We still lived in our trailer home, but our dream house stood beside it, framed and enclosed. Michael came home every day and transformed from mail carrier to carpenter with just a quick change of clothes. He walked, on average, 11 miles every day delivering mail, but every night he hammered and sawed until, exhausted, he toppled into bed and went unconscious. I swept up sawdust and picked up stray nails. I wanted to help more, but with a three-year-old and newborn, I wasn't able to do much.

As the weather turned nice again, the four of us spent more time involved with the construction. Mike did the meaningful, productive work. Eric followed his dad everywhere and continuously handed him assorted tools. "Thanks, Dude," Michael said, as he set the tools aside. "We'll use that one in a little bit." Eric was proud to be 'helping' his dad. Rebecca was shuffled here and there on the plywood sub-flooring in her little Nip Nap seat, while she discovered her tiny pink fists and kicked her booties off. She was a sweet-tempered and patient baby.

We sold our trailer and moved into our house in November of 1973. Eric was almost 4 and Becki was 9 months old. We didn't have the heat installed yet, so the four of us slept in front of the huge fieldstone fireplace that Michael and I built on one wall of the living room. Mike continued to do finish work.

We had two beautiful kids, a brand new home and Mike had a good job, but still Mom took issue with so many things in our life. I was often impatient with her. I wanted so badly for her and Michael to get along. Even silly things like painting the rooms in the house were cause for a war of words. Mike pried open a gallon of paint and began to stir. "You're not painting the living room *that* color, are you?" she said with disgust.

"Yup, we are. We both picked out this color. If you don't like it then maybe you shouldn't come around. You can pick the colors for your own house, not ours." Michael said. I prayed that an all out war would not ensue. He simply would not tolerate her attempts to cause discord in our lives. Later Mike and I clashed when I suggested he not be so brutal with my mother. They were both obstinate and opinionated. And as always, I was in the middle, trying to mediate.

Jeanne Wilhite Dunn

The righteous care for the needs of their animals,
but the kindest acts of the wicked are cruel.
Proverbs 12:10

Chapter 26

This morning our granddaughter, Tabitha and I go to the barn to groom the horses. Tabitha is Becki's older daughter and is a natural around horses. Michael's team of Haflinger draft horses and Willow, the old saddle horse we bought for Tabbie and the other grandchildren, are the only horses we have now. Our rescue donkey, Tulip, shares the big barn with the horses.

I taught Tabbie to ride when she was a little girl. Now at 17 years old, she is an excellent equestrian, gentle, confident, and skilled. She leads Willow out of the barn so we can gently work the currycomb and brush over his bony body.

As I run my hand along his graceful neck, I decide we are alike in many ways. He and I are both showing our age. Tabbie carefully brushes over the big scar on his flank where he was branded in his former life out west. He is living his last years here on Frog Hollow Homestead. He is rarely ridden anymore and I certainly don't ride like I did when I was young. As we soothe Willow's aging frame with the brush, I remember a horse named Marni and my mother's view of my horsemanship.

*****

I had just returned from a riding lesson and was busy unhitching the horse trailer in the driveway. Mom drove in, blocking our Jeep in, so I was unable to drive the vehicle away from the trailer hitch. "Mom, can you back up so I can move the Jeep?" I called. I wondered if she had blocked me in deliberately. She obliged and Emily, our shaggy farm dog ambassador, met her as she got out of her car. "Thanks, Mom. Marni and I had a dressage lesson this morning," I said, leaning against the Jeep. My riding boots and helmet sat next to the driveway in the grass. "I just unloaded her," I said, motioning to the Palomino horse that was bolting through the pasture behind us.

"You mean to tell me that you truck the horse all the way to that stable, just to ride her over there? Are you crazy?" I was excited and happy to be taking dressage and hunt seat lessons on my own horse, but suddenly my joy was waning.

"Yes Mom, I do. And no I am not crazy."

"Oh yes you are! When are you going to outgrow this foolishness? Sooner or later you're going to get hurt messing around with these big animals."

"I have to move the Jeep," I answered, ignoring her remark. As I climbed into the seat, I realized that she meant to say something like, Jeanne, I am so fearful that you might get hurt riding those big horses. I don't want anything to happen to you because I love you. However, that is not what came out of her mouth.

I loved riding and Marni was a spirited horse. I knew there was an inherent risk involved in horseback riding, but I loved it anyway. Perhaps I enjoyed the feeling of controlling something bigger and stronger than me. This was one thing I had power and control over.

We had filled up our barns. In addition to our own horses, we boarded others, had a small herd of dairy goats, chickens, ducks, barn cats and our wonderful family dog, Emily. Mom loved the animals, especially Emily. She watched the chickens peck at corn and even brought them vegetables and greens as a treat. She often leaned over the goat yard fence to pat the does on the head when they came to the fence to greet her.

So why did she try to discourage me from keeping animals? That was the ambiguity of my mother. She was hard to figure out. I continued to learn how to pick my battles and avoid the landmines. Sometimes it took all of my strength to resist my mother's control and I used to joke with Mike saying, "Mom is on her way down here. I just changed into my suit of armor." I was willing to ignore her sarcastic remarks, but Mike refused. That caused quarrels and disputes between us.

My repulsive thumb habit continued like an addiction. Putting my thumb in my mouth was an awful coping mechanism. When I felt out of control and wanted to feel secure, I positioned my thumb in my mouth and grabbed for the closest fabric I could find to rub on my nose or lip. I hated myself for seeking relief in this juvenile manner. God, please take this sickening curse from me, I prayed tearfully. What is wrong with you, I asked myself with utter disgust. But I kept doing it.

> Above all else, guard your heart,
> for it is the wellspring of life.
> Proverb 4:23

Chapter 27

  It's the Christmas season once again. Our parents have been gone for well over ten years. The only family we have close by are the Truelsons, Rebecca, her husband Eric, and Tabitha and Kylie. Our Christmases are quieter now and that is a welcome treat. It gives us more time to reflect on our Savior's birth. Our tree is trimmed and the house is decorated with things that have been in our family for more than 45 years. On Saturday, Rebecca, the girls and I will gather for our annual Christmas cookie baking tradition. I wish our Tennessee grandkids, Eric's children, Chelsea and Nick, could be a part of it. Eric is remarried now and we have two step-grandkids as well, Gabriel and Carly. Christmas is my favorite time of the year. I remember a Christmas long before we had any grandchildren. It was a Christmas that Eric and Rebecca were too young to remember. And that was a good thing.

*****

Holidays were difficult. Eric and Rebecca had both maternal and paternal grandparents who wanted to see them on Christmas. It was an annual aggravation for me to plan holiday visits. We really did try to be fair, but both Michael's parents and mine never seemed happy with the arrangement. "You're going to be with his people on Christmas morning?" was my mother's condescending remark. She found it distasteful to even say Mike's name.

"Yes Mom, and you make it sound like they are from outer space."

We tried inviting everyone to our house for Christmas dinner, but the Dunns and Wilhites had a strained relationship at best. We pulled it off a few times during the children's school age years, but it was uncomfortable for everyone. We all could have taken a lesson from the men in the family. The dads always shook hands in greeting, called one another by their names, and chatted comfortably about a multitude of topics. The women, me included, couldn't wait to get away from one another. The mothers' relationship was forced and conversation was stiff. The atmosphere was as tense as a rubber band stretched across the dining room table. Michael's mother was grumpy because she was forced to be in my mother's presence and my mother was fuming because she had to share me with my mother-in-law. Thank God, the children created a buffer zone. Everybody loved them and they were an easy focal point for conversation and attention.

When the children were toddlers, I experienced the most wretched Christmas Day in my memory. I was feeling despondent after hearing about a particularly unpleasant exchange between Mike and my mother. Apparently, she had suggested to Mike that they each buy a charm to add to my charm bracelet for Christmas. According to my husband, my mother got bossy in the jewelry store, embarrassed him and he walked out without purchasing a charm. According to my mother, who made sure I heard her side of the story too, Michael embarrassed her and argued about who was going to give which charm. After the tussle, there were no charms at all under the Christmas tree for me.

However, something of much greater consequence developed from that silly skirmish in the jewelry store. It fueled the ever-smoldering flames of resentment. The smoldering embers in the battle of wills ignited again. The phone rang on Christmas Eve.

"Ooo, maybe it's Santa Claus, Eric!" I said, raising my eyebrows and smiling mysteriously. Both Eric and Rebecca ran to the phone as I picked it up. I tried to make the holidays as magical and fun as my parents did when I was little. "Hello and Merry Christmas!" I announced and winked at the kids.

"Hello Jeanne. It's Mom. Listen, you and the kids are invited to come tomorrow for Christmas dinner, but that man is not." I could not find words to respond. I wrinkled my nose and shook my head at the little ones who clung to my legs.

"Not Santa," I mouthed, trying to camouflage my shock.

She spoke again, "I don't want him around our family." My throat tightened as though someone had wrapped a strangulation cord around my neck. Choose between us. Who do you love more, Jeanne? Make your choice.

Before I suffocated completely, I managed to avoid and redirect, my survival tactic. "I have to go, Mom. The kids are spilling their hot cocoa," I lied.

I got very little sleep that Christmas Eve. While the world grew silent in awe of the Savior born that holy night, I cried and prayed that God would somehow take this torment from me. I was in the middle once again and, because I loved them both, I agonized over what to do the following day. Mike was noncommittal when I asked him what he thought I should do. "It's your decision," was all he said. I felt like the kids and I were being used as pawns in an irrational contest. I took the children to my parents' house late on Christmas morning, but refused to stay for dinner.

"But I cooked all this food," my mother whimpered. I knew how dedicated my mom was to her family. She spent hours and used the best of ingredients when cooking for her loved ones. I felt like a hardhearted Scrooge, but felt I couldn't wait any longer to get back to where I belonged, home to Michael, who was sitting alone on Christmas Day without his wife and children.

Jeanne Wilhite Dunn

> For God so loved the world that he gave his one and only Son, that whoever believes in him shall not perish but have eternal life.
> John 3:16

Chapter 28

I made friends with several of our neighbors on North Court Street. Spring arrived after Rebecca's birth and I popped her in her carriage and walked the children down the road to visit. One neighbor, Diane, had a little boy the same age as Eric. She and I visited often while our little ones played together. The conversation always seemed to come around to her faith and salvation in Jesus Christ. Each time I left her house I considered her beliefs and wondered how she could be so sure of her religious convictions. She always had an open Bible on the dining room table. How could she muddle through all the strange words and phrases in that thing? Maybe she didn't really read it, but left it there for show. No, I reasoned, she not only read it, but actually studied it, because she could quote some of the verses from memory. She seemed to have a special joy and love for her Jesus that I couldn't quite understand.

One day I received a letter from Cathy, my old high school friend, who had joined Campus Crusade for Christ. Her letter explained that she had accepted Jesus as her Lord and Savior. Her words sounded familiar and very much like the words of Diane down the street. Suddenly it seemed everywhere I turned someone was talking about salvation or the Bible. I had the uncanny feeling that something supernatural was happening to me. Was this Jesus real? Why did people continually pester me about Him?

Curious, I decided to read the Bible I had been given by my Sunday school teachers long ago. I found it, collecting dust upstairs in the closet. I opened it. The first page I set my eyes on was in the book of Revelation and I was instantly drawn to the red lettering, "Here I am! I stand at the door and knock. If anyone hears my voice and opens the door, I will come in and eat with that person, and they with me." (Rev.3:20 The NIV Study Bible) I slammed the black book shut and moved away from it warily. What was happening to me? The words were so powerful, I felt like the God of the universe had literally spoken. I paced around the house, talking to myself. This is crazy. Am I losing my mind? This couldn't be a coincidence, could it? I was unable to get the powerful words out of my mind. Was Jesus knocking on the door of my heart? I knew He was talking to me, just as I knew the sun rose over the barn every morning. But I was too stubborn and scared to answer Him.

What do you want with me, God? I knew my Bible stories. "Who can tell me what David used to slay Goliath?" Mrs. Sheffield asked our third grade Sunday school class.

My hand shot up and I shouted out the answer before she called on me, "One smooth stone and a sling shot!"

My dad drove Lynn and me to Sunday school every week while we were in elementary and middle school. Our parents only went to the Sunday service on Christmas and Easter, but Lynn and I knew all about the old Presbyterian Church, including all the secret hiding places and how to get to the belfry.

Every Sunday morning we colored in our workbooks, listened to amazing Bible stories like Jonah and the whale and baby Moses floating down the Nile River in a basket. We memorized the Lord's Prayer and learned the words to "Jesus Loves Me," thanks to our dedicated teachers. It never occurred to me that the Bible was literally the inspired word of God. I just enjoyed hearing the outlandish stories. Nor did I realize that one day I would have a real personal relationship with Jesus Christ.

I was getting tired of my neighbor, Diane, asking me to her church service all the time. She put it a different way each time she asked,

"Want to come to church with me on Sunday morning?"

"Nope."

"I just thought I'd call to invite you to come see what my church is like. You'd love the music."

"No, thanks. I'm busy."

"Why don't you come to the Sunday night worship service with me? You would love Pastor Bates. Come on, try it."

After endless prodding, I finally decided that I would accompany her to the next Sunday night worship service.

"I think you're all crazy," I told Diane, "and if I get the opportunity, I think I'm going to tell your minister exactly that. And I might ask him some tough questions." Bizarre events were happening in my life and I wanted to find out why. My strategy was to lash out because I felt so helpless and confused. My threat didn't seem to bother her in the least.

I walked into the tiny chapel near Oneida Lake and plopped down in a pew next to Diane. There were a dozen or so people scattered in the seats. As soon as he spotted me, Pastor Roger Bates, approached me and shook my hand vigorously. "We're so happy to have you with us and Jesus is too! God bless you real good now," he smiled. He was a small man with a bald head and glasses, but Pastor Bates was genuine and friendly and I liked him right away. His warm and welcoming charm put me at ease immediately and I felt at home.

After he led the small congregation in a rousing version of the gospel song, "Power in the Blood," I remembered my plan. I was there to prove this minister and his congregation were over-zealous quacks. I raised my hand to ask a loaded question and forgot my own name. I simply could not speak. Pastor Bates asked if I wanted him to pray for me. I nodded my head and moved to the altar before him. I began to cry spontaneously as Pastor Bates prayed. I heard his voice, a thousand miles away, ask if I wanted to accept Jesus Christ as my Lord and Savior. As the Holy Spirit hovered around me in this tiny church, I prayed the sinner's prayer. At 24 years old, I was reborn and became a daughter of the Most High God. I didn't need to know a bunch of scripture and I didn't need to have lived a sinless life. All I needed was to ask forgiveness for my sins and allow Jesus to fill my heart with His love. "Therefore, if anyone is in Christ, the new creation has come: The old has gone, the new is here!" (2 Cor. 5:17) I was indeed, a new creature!

I went home and tried to explain to Michael the supernatural, holy encounter I had experienced. No wonder my Christian friends talked so much about Jesus! They wanted to share the good news of salvation and now I did too. I pestered Mike for several weeks, sharing Bible passages and reporting answers to prayer. I tried to explain the love, joy and peace I felt, gifts of the Holy Spirit, I told Mike. I knew that eternal life with the Lord was mine and I wanted that for Michael, too. The Holy Spirit began to speak to my husband, despite my pathetic attempt to explain the things of God. Within a few months, Michael too, experienced the life-changing phenomenon of accepting Jesus Christ as his Lord and Savior.

We were out of the woods! We surrendered our lives to God and knew that He was in control. We thought that since we had become Christians all the problems in our life would just fade away. Oops, that was wrong! I began studying my Bible daily and came upon a passage in Exodus that would cause me to agonize over my relationship with my mother for years to come. It read, "Honor your father and your mother, so that you may live long in the land the Lord your God is giving you."

(Exodus 20:12) I had learned the Ten Commandments as a child. Why had I forgotten this one?

Church became an integral part of our lives and we were so thankful that our children would be raised in a Christian home, not a perfect home, for none of us was perfect, but they would have an understanding of the verse from Joshua 24:15, "But as for me and my household, we will serve the Lord."

As the years passed, there were times of peace and times of strife in our family. The years had been a friend to me as I learned, day by day, to lean on God for my strength. I discovered that it was right in God's eyes for me to cling to my husband, even if I had to forsake all others. Our marriage grew stronger and I knew it was because God was the center of our marriage. "Though one may be overpowered, two can defend themselves. A cord of three strands is not quickly broken." (Ecclesiastes 4:12) Mike and I were two strands, but that third strand was God and His strength held us together.

Jeanne Wilhite Dunn

> Gracious words are a honeycomb,
> sweet to the soul and healing to the bones.
> Proverbs 16:24

Chapter 29

Mom and Dad had their hands full raising my brothers, who were now teenagers. In fact, when things began to unravel at their house and the boys rebelled, my parents called us to come over and intervene. We joked that my parents were so busy with my younger brothers that they didn't have time to interfere in our lives. Jamie was easily agitated and had a quick temper and redheaded Mikey reminded us of me when I was his age. He was strong-willed, knew what was important to him and devised ways to get what he wanted, including a car.

Surprisingly, both my parents began attending church regularly. Eventually my father became a trustee and Mom taught junior high Sunday school. Her students adored her. I was glad that my parents were seeking God.

At home on Frog Hollow Homestead, our life together had settled into a peaceable kingdom in many ways. Eric and Becki were now school age and were a constant source of pride. They were good students and busy with music, sports, and friends. We bought 30 acres of woods across the street and spent many hours there as a family, cutting and collecting firewood, hiking and picnicking. At home, we had flower and vegetable gardens, hobbies, and an amusing assortment of farm animals to enjoy. Over the years, we surrounded ourselves with all the things we loved, and our farm was our sanctuary.

Best of all, I stopped sucking my thumb. I awoke one day to the realization that I had not sucked my thumb in months. The craving had simply vanished! I hadn't even thought about it and this revelation was hard to believe. When had I stopped? I didn't even know. God had worked a secret miracle in my life and my enslavement was gone! I put my thumb in my mouth, just as doubting Thomas put his fingers in Jesus' nail-scarred hands and His side. It was awkward and my thumb tasted foreign and bitter. I rejoiced alone, for to share this shameful secret with anyone but God was unthinkable. I would never again have any desire to use my thumb for comfort. I had God as my Comforter and He had set me free!

Jeanne Wilhite Dunn

Let someone else praise you, and not your own mouth;
an outsider, and not your own lips.
Proverbs 27:2

Chapter 30

Michael and I hoe between the Roma tomato plants in our garden. We love to get up early and work in the garden before the summer sun begins to roast the day. It is still cool and we have already picked a pot of raspberries and filled the wheelbarrow with zucchini and yellow squash. We are quiet. There is no need to talk, for we commune and heal working the good earth. Now that we are older we have reduced the size of the plot, but decades of adding organic material and manure help our soil to yield plenty. We will share what we cannot eat. We have taken pleasure and benefit from a garden for as long as I can remember.

*****

Early one Saturday morning my mother pulled into the gravel driveway, the tires crunching stones and pebbles like a steamroller. Emily barked twice to alert me that someone had arrived. I stood up in the garden and stretched my back. "Hi Mom!" I called, stepping over the row of beans I had just finished weeding. Mom stopped to greet Emily and scratched her head affectionately. She loved cats and dogs as much as I did and I heard her talking baby gibberish to Em. "What's up today?" I asked, as I brushed the soil from my hands. She picked her way toward me and paused at the edge of the garden. I rustled through the green bean plants and offered up a long green bean still wet from the morning dew. "Look Mom! I have fresh beans," I crowed. We had planted tomatoes, corn, cucumbers and summer squash, in addition to the green beans, and everything was flourishing.

"Why do you bother with all this," she replied, sweeping her arm widely over our vegetable patch, "when you can buy any vegetable you want at the grocery store?" Crestfallen, I bit down on my green bean and stared at my mother. Why do I allow her remarks to bother me?

Often, when I felt she was trying to plant doubt in my mind as she was doing now, I deliberately tried to lighten the air with a funny comeback. "Because Mom, I love to get dirty!" I chuckled, "Don't you remember when I used to play in the dirt pile?" Avoid and redirect was my relationship survival strategy. Sometimes it worked. She ignored my attempt at humor and patted Emily, who was nosing her hand for more attention.

After what I judged to be an obvious attempt to criticize my lifestyle, I could have easily gotten defensive. But what was the use? We exchanged so many unkind words in the past. I tried to avoid confrontations about the little things. It never occurred to me that maybe she was genuinely concerned about my working in the hot sun. I was prone to migraine headaches and she knew that the hot sun beating down on my head often triggered one. Besides, as a city girl, she thought a garden was a lot of unnecessary work.

"I'm on my way to the store. Do you want me to pick up anything for you?" she asked, turning back toward her car. She could be so thoughtful yet so intimidating in the same moment.

"No, but thanks for thinking of me," I replied as I walked beside her.

"My knees are killing me," she complained. Over the years, arthritis had affected her knees and her legs had begun to bow slightly. She was in constant pain and rocked from side to side when she walked. When we reached her car, she turned suddenly. "Oh yes, Aunt Margaret and Uncle Will are coming up next Saturday," she announced. She got into her car, turned the key in the ignition, and added, "I'll bring them down." I waved goodbye. Downhearted, I trudged inside to shower. Somehow, I didn't feel like working in the garden anymore.

Whenever her family and friends visited from Long Island or New York City, Mom always brought them to our farm. The gardens, barnyard and farm equipment seemed to disgust her until company came. Then Mom and Dad would show up with people by the carloads.

The following weekend, as expected, they arrived with Aunt Margaret, Uncle Will and their adult special needs son, Billy. Emily announced their arrival by barking and wagging her tail furiously. She approached Uncle Will as he got out of the car and wiped her wet whiskered nose on his baby blue leisure suit. Mom hopped out of the car with gusto and began chattering about how Michael had built the house and barn by himself. She toured the place with family in tow and boasted about our gardens, the flock of chickens, and even the fish in the pond.

"Jeanne," she called, "Billy can fish in your pond, right?" I nodded from the porch steps, embarrassed by her bragging.

"It's stocked with sunfish, small-mouth bass and bullhead," she continued. "And they have a Blue Heron who comes to the pond and helps himself to their fish," she laughed. I didn't realize she knew so much about our pond. Dad, Uncle Will and Michael chatted easily under the sycamore tree in the backyard. Part of me did enjoy her boasting about our home and lifestyle, but I couldn't help but wonder if she was looking for positive strokes and acceptance for herself on some level. Maybe she really was proud of what Michael and I had accomplished. I chose to believe so.

On another occasion when her long time friends from boarding school were visiting, she brought them at milking time in the goat barn. She gushed on and on about how we raised the goats, milked them by hand and made cheese. While Mom did love the animals themselves, she thought we were crazy for putting up with all the work that was required to keep them. Baling hay, shoveling manure, and birthing kids were nothing my mother would ever get involved with. But I thrived in this environment and knew this was the life I was meant to live. In fact, I thanked God every day for the fulfilling life He gave me.

"Wait til you see what they've done with the house, Alyce!" Mom left me to finish milking the goats and led Alyce to the house. As I came in with the stainless steel pail half full of frothy milk, I heard my mother in our bedroom. "Jeanne made this quilt by hand. Just look at the stitching." Alyce fussed over the quilt, but Mom was on to other things. "They just redecorated and wallpapered the bathroom. Check this out! Isn't it adorable?" It was difficult for my mother to compliment Mike and me directly, but I learned what pleased her during the annual visits from the city folks. And she basked in the reflective glory of a daughter and son-in-law who had made their dreams come true.

Mom and Michael had periods of time when they ceased the fighting and bickering. Those times were like heaven to me. But those interludes never lasted long. I knew I was mired down in a tangled web of unhealthy actions and reactions from the people around me and it was a painful existence. It was not an easy path and it took me years to learn that my self-worth was not dependent on my mother's opinion, but on how God saw me. I also learned that we all have struggles and tribulations in life. My mother's challenge was trying to raise a family, without the benefit of a secure, happy childhood herself. She had nothing from which to draw any parenting skills.

Nor did my father. He never even knew his parents or what it meant to be part of a family. And parenting certainly did not come with an instruction manual.

Jeanne Wilhite Dunn

Why are you downcast, O my soul? Why so disturbed
within me? Put your hope in God,
for I will yet praise him, my Savior and my God.
Psalm 42:5

Chapter 31

A friend stops by today for a cup of tea. We talk about the weather, always a safe subject, and her job and family. Finally, after the small talk, she gains enough courage to tell me about her struggle with depression. I am older now and young women often ask for advice or just an ear to listen. I take pleasure in this, as it validates me as a person with some insight. And my friends know their secrets are safe with me.

As I talk with her, the conversation reminds me of my own dark days when I was in my twenties. I pray that God will give me the wisdom and the words to help my dear friend during this difficult time. I remember thinking I would never again feel sunshine on my face or hope in my heart.

*****

I was becoming emotionally exhausted and crippled from years of conflict between Michael and my mother. I knew, as time went on, that she was desperate for love and acceptance. Keeping her family intact was paramount in her mind. It seemed that because she never received the love and security she needed as a child, she was hanging on to her kids, or at least me. Her tenacity was crushing the life out of me. She needed to keep us all in check, but I was the maverick who broke her heart, by resisting her controlling ways. My growing up and leaving her was a critical blow.

I began to feel sick all the time. My stomach churned continuously and migraine headaches were a common occurrence. I cared for the children, but anything beyond that seemed like an insurmountable task. I stopped caring if the house was clean or how I looked. I refused to answer the telephone or leave the house. I was disgusted with myself. After all, I had so many blessings in my life; I had no reason at all to be depressed. I was a child of God. I was ashamed that I snapped at Mike and the children so much. Any shred of self-esteem had vanished and everything began to seem meaningless. I felt like I was sinking into black quicksand.

I continued to spiral downward until I began having night terrors. I had reoccurring nightmares and would wake from horrible dreams, screaming and thrashing. Mike turned the lights on and I awoke, hearing his voice as he tried to reassure me. Even though I was awake, I still saw monstrous people and snakes in our bedroom. The terror and panic were real. The dreams came nightly and took on a life of their own and we were frightened that I could not differentiate between reality and dream. We decided to seek help.

Our family doctor advised me to see a psychiatrist. I did so and discovered with Dr. Morrow's help, that I was experiencing anger that I had turned inward upon myself. I thought it was too dangerous to direct my anger at other people in my life. I had tried to keep peace in the family and worn myself into a tattered rag. I was angry at Michael and I was angry with my mother. Without even being conscious of it, I discovered that deep down I felt I was a very bad person for growing up and leaving my mother. The road back from the darkness and pain in my life was not easy.

During psychotherapy, I began to believe that everyone would be better off without me. Dr. Morrow could use his time on someone else, a patient who was more valuable than I was. Mike and my mother would no longer have a reason to fight, and, best of all, my profound pain would go away. When I mumbled my idea at one of my therapy sessions, Dr. Morrow ordered medication and insisted that I take it.

I was embarrassed to be on medication. What would my Christian friends say if they knew? Would they say I was depressed because I didn't have enough faith? Maybe they would accuse me of allowing Satan to get a foothold in my life. What kind of a Christian needs a psychiatrist and mind-altering drugs? I wanted desperately to isolate myself, especially from church. I took my medication every day and within a couple of weeks, I began to notice a change. The sun began peeking from behind the clouds in my life. I realized God was good even though I experienced heartache in my life. Three years of outpatient psychiatric care helped me to cope. As the years passed, I finally learned how to function independently of my mother and release many of the negative feelings I had about not conforming to her wishes and expectations.

I started reading my Bible again. I asked God to help me focus on the blessings in my life, rather than the problems. I began to pray in desperation daily that Michael and my Mom would at least come to accept each other. She and Michael argued and fought. I tried to referee and often begged Michael to ignore her snide remarks. Throughout our kids' childhoods there were months on end when they did not see their grandparents because something had angered my Mom. Then she would suddenly change her mind and Michael would be in her good graces, but only for a season. This made for dreadful holidays and caused me tremendous pain and anxiety.

In September 1978, Rebecca got on the school bus for kindergarten for the first time with her big brother, Eric. It was a day of reckoning for me. I squinted through the camera lens and prompted the kids to smile before they climbed on the bus. I waved goodbye frantically, hoping my tears would abate. I stood there at the end of the driveway and felt bewildered. Suddenly I felt I no longer had a purpose in life. Who would I feed and teach and nurture during the days now? Both our children were off to spend happy days with their teachers and friends. I felt like I had been abandoned and left behind. Had my own mother felt this way? Teary-eyed, I walked past the barn, knowing no matter how many animals we acquired, they would never fulfill the deep need I had to provide and protect.

Michael and I spent many hours talking about my feelings of discontent. "Do you think I should go back to school?" I asked. Dr Morrow had suggested doing so might give me a new healthy challenge, instead of dwelling on the issues with my mother.

Michael had reservations. "What if you fall in love with one of the professors?" he joked, but I knew there was a touch of real uncertainty in his remark.

The following January, I enrolled in a college nearby to pursue an education to become a teacher. When Eric and Becki eagerly returned to school after Christmas break, I began classes too. I was anxious to share my decision with my parents. I was sure that they would be elated that after almost a decade, I was indeed getting that college education that they wanted so badly for me. But Mom reacted with skepticism, "How in the world do you expect to go to college with two kids and a husband?" I made up some simple response and left.

During my second year, I sat in the guidance office at school waiting to be called in. I had been taking liberal arts classes and needed to start thinking about classes specifically for an education major. As I waited, I noticed a stack of pamphlets on the table beside me. I looked away, but was drawn back again and again until finally I picked one up. It was a brochure about the nursing program at the college. As I read the information, I had the distinct feeling that I was hearing the supernatural voice of God, "This is what I want you to do with your life, Jeanne. My will is that you become a nurse." I heard the words as clearly as if another person in the room had spoken them. I looked around the waiting room to be sure I was the only one there. A nurse? That was down near the bottom of my list of desirable careers. I had never even entertained the idea before. When the counselor called me to her office, I asked about the nursing curriculum, trying to sound as though I was just curious. On the 30-minute drive home, I prayed continually, Oh God, I am terrible in math. I could never stick a needle into anyone. People make me nervous. I don't like the smell of hospitals.

God chuckled, and spoke into my heart, "I know, Jeanne. Trust me." I knew undeniably that I would change my major and the direction of my life. Nursing school was difficult. When I got A's and B's in every class, I knew it was because I had chosen to do God's will. After three and a half long years, I graduated with honors. After graduating from nursing school, I took the state examination and become a licensed professional registered nurse.

I would spend the next 34 years in a rewarding nursing career in a local hospital. I had thought teaching would be something I would enjoy. But my Heavenly Father had a divine plan for me. I spent the first 17 years of my career as a bedside nurse on a medical-surgical unit. I loved caring for the patients there. It fulfilled my need to nurture and care for others. Then God presented an opportunity and I became the Staff Development Coordinator for the hospital. In this position, I was responsible for training newly hired nurses and providing education for the clinical staff at the hospital. Instead of caring for patients, I was responsible for caring for the caregivers. I became both nurse and teacher! God knew what He was doing!

He heals the brokenhearted and
binds up their wounds. Psalm 147:3

Chapter 32

Michael and I had been married for nearly ten years. We sometimes wondered if our marriage had been successful because we were driven to prove my mother wrong. Maybe it was possible that love really did conquer all and we simply had a marriage made in heaven. The reality was that God was the center of our lives and our marriage. It was not an easy ten years by any means. Michael and I were convinced that, because we had married so young, we had finished growing up together and melded into one.

Since our tenth wedding anniversary was coming, we decided it was the perfect time to renew our marriage vows. Now that we knew Jesus as our personal Savior, it would be particularly meaningful to renew our wedding vows again as Christians. Michael and I were frightened young brats when we married the first time. This ceremony would be different. We would share this happy day with those we loved most, our entire families. I shared the happy news of the upcoming celebration with my parents. I thought I saw my mother bristle slightly, like an injured alley cat, but I shrugged it off. Eric and Rebecca could be our attendants this time. They were 9 and 6 years old respectively and were excited at the prospect.

I set to work making handmade invitations. The ceremony would take place at our church, the tiny chapel near the lake, where we first gave our hearts and lives to Jesus. We knew and loved Pastor Bates there. We felt the Holy Spirit at work in the little chapel and it was our home church.

We enlisted the help of Mike's musical cousins to play the organ and sing solos. I spent hours making silk flower arrangements for the altar and flower head wreaths for Becki and me. I spent more time making my dress, Rebecca's dress and forest green velvet vests for Eric and his dad to wear. The floor-length dresses were fashioned from polished cotton in a tiny earth-tone print. We looked kind of like a hippy family, all four of our outfits either matching or coordinating in some way.

A good friend helped me to make food in advance for the party we would host in our home after the ceremony. I felt that God was giving me the opportunity to experience some of the wedding day joys that we had missed ten years ago. Most important to me was the presence and blessing of my mother and father and the fact that we could rededicate our lives to each other and to God. I thanked God as I joyfully prepared for this special day. I felt all would be made right in my troubled heart.

Most of the guests responded and were happy to let us know that they would be there for the ceremony. We had not heard from my parents and I began to feel uneasy. My sister and her family had moved away to Florida and I knew she would not be able to attend, but certainly, my parents and brothers would come. I wiped my hands on my apron and put the big pan of Swedish meatballs I was working on in the refrigerator. I dialed Mom's number. "Hi, Mom! I just wanted to make sure that you and Dad and the boys are coming when we renew our marriage vows next Saturday night. I didn't hear back from you. Did you see on the invitation that you're all invited back to our house for a party?"

Silence on the other end of the line caused me to talk faster as my anxiety heightened. "Lorna has been down here every day this week, helping me make all the food. I just finished making 200 Swedish meatballs." The silence on the other end of the phone was lethal. "Mom?"

Finally she spoke. "Why are you doing this? Just to torment and disgrace your father and I a little bit more?" she said. I was speechless. It never occurred to me that she would respond in this way. We had not intended to offend anyone, but it was obvious that my mother was hurt and angry. I had opened an old wound. How silly of me to think that enough healing had taken place in ten years. In fact, how ridiculous it was to think that our dysfunctional family would ever be healed and whole.

She continued, "Listen, we'll come. But you and your friends can celebrate without us afterwards. Jeanne, as far as I'm concerned, the day you married that man was the day you died." I was stunned.

"So you're just coming to the church, right?" I asked, trying to speak calmly and clearly before the lump in my throat gave way to tears.

She confirmed my conclusion and I quickly responded, "I've gotta go now. Bye." With her statement, I realized the depth of anguish and sorrow in my mother's heart. I cried for myself and for her. Through a flood of tears, I told myself over and over again that I would not let this ruin our ceremony. I prayed that God would restore her and help her to let go of the past. It was then that I realized that I too, needed to let go of the hurt.

The renewal of our marriage vows was a lovely affair. The chapel, glowing with candlelight and beautiful music, was crowded with our friends and family. Mom, Dad, Jamie and Mikey came in and sat near the back. My brothers were getting so big. I noticed that Mikey was almost as tall as Dad was. Pastor Bates greeted them all with a hearty handshake, just as he did with all of our guests. I hoped that they would feel the love and joy that I was experiencing that evening. I suppose Mom and Dad felt they had done their duty and conceded, so they slipped out before Mike and I and the children had a chance to thank them for coming. In my heart I knew that I had been unsuccessful in attempting to find what had been missing 10 years ago, my parents' approval. We returned to Frog Hollow Homestead to rejoice with friends who loved us as a couple. I smiled for photographs and laughed at the funny things Mike and our friends said that night, but my heart was broken with disappointment.

Mike and Mom's relationship was always on rocky ground. How silly I was to think that once I became a Christian all the problems in my life would just fade into oblivion. I tried frantically to please my husband and my mother. I was constantly torn and forced to make a choice between the two of them. I tried to keep peace, but they butted heads just like a couple of angry mountain goats. This went on for years. I knew I was to honor my mother, but it was so difficult when she was making my life so rotten. God spoke to me often and reminded me that I needed to find forgiveness in my heart for my parents for refusing to come to our wedding.

Life went on and I tried to forget the telephone conversation with my mother before our anniversary celebration. She and Dad occasionally stopped by for coffee when they were out. Mike and I sipped tea while we all sat around the dining room table and chatted about the weather. Our dog, Emily, the ultimate peacemaker, loved Mom and always put her head gently on Mom's lap. Mom scratched the wiry hair on Emily's chin and gave her little treats from the table. Harmony reigned at our dining room table! I treasured the times when the lion would lay down with the lamb. All was well.

> Blessed are those who mourn,
> for they will be comforted.
> Matthew 5:4

Chapter 33

Then a tragedy, beyond anything our family could ever imagine, occurred. When the call came just after midnight, I rushed to the hospital where I worked, the first to learn that our youngest brother, Mikey, had been killed in a car accident, along with two teenage girls. By the time I reached my mom and dad, the police had delivered the horrific news to them in person. Mike and the kids and I convened at Mom and Dad's where we sat on the floor in their living room, too numb to even speak. Mom did not cry, but silently stared at the tissue she held in her lap. Even when I patted her hand and asked if she was all right, she continued to stare and would not speak. I was worried about her.

Dad sat at the kitchen table, drank coffee and wiped his tears with the back of his hand. My brother, Jamie was the only one who spoke. His coping skills were minimal and he was easily agitated. He wandered from room to room talking to himself. We sat together in shock and disbelief through the cruel night until dawn arrived. It was Easter morning but grief shrouded us and I knew there would be nothing but darkness for our family that day.

"Mom, the sun is up. Will you go for a walk with me?" I asked gently. She had been nearly motionless for hours. We walked together up Stroud Street, huddled together against the chill of early spring. A cardinal sang his liquid melody, breaking our sad silence. The sun rose, turning the sky Easter pink. The bitter night had spent itself and we wobbled our way along the street. Arm in arm, we leaned into each other as though just being upright was too much to bear. We stared at the pavement in front of our shoes as we stumbled along, too numb, too blind to even lift our eyes. Silence followed us, but I felt closer to my mother than I ever thought possible. We moved slowly toward home, breathing in the fresh morning air, hoping against hope to sweep this nightmare and heartache away. Mikey was only 18.

"It's Easter morning, Mom." I whispered softly.

She stopped dead in her tracks and turned to look at me. "Mikey's gone." She said flatly.

After the funeral, Mike and I looked in on my parents often. They appeared to have grown old and withered. When either of them talked about Mikey and cried, I was strong, held them close, and did my best to comfort them. When I thought of my handsome, redheaded kid brother and began to sob uncontrollably, my mother flew to my side and offered her strength and wisdom. We all took turns shoring up whoever needed it the most at any given moment.

Jeanne Wilhite Dunn

> I have hidden your word in my heart
> that I might not sin against you.
> Psalm 119:11

Chapter 34

Today is spring-cleaning day in the happy house that Michael built for us over four decades ago. I lovingly scrub and clean, one of my favorite things to do at home. I begin dusting our bedroom, decorated with the treasures we obtained from a trip to Africa a few years ago. We brought back a small collection of hand-carved African animals from our safari in Kenya.

There in the midst of the artfully carved wooden beasts, there is a glass giraffe from the local dollar store. I carefully take it to the sink to be washed and dried. It was the last gift we received from my mother before her death. The giraffe had lowered her long neck to tend to her baby, who stood safely beside her. I wonder if Mom selected it because she knew we loved animals or because it represented a mother/daughter bond. Either way, she had picked it out without thought of its monetary worth.

Before she got sick, as a creative and discriminate shopper, she would never have dreamed of shopping in the dollar store for a gift. But that is what made it all the more precious to me.

I miss my mom. After all, it was through my relationship with her that I would finally put my hope in God. "Why are you downcast, O my soul? Why so disturbed within me? Put your hope in God, for I will yet praise him, my Savior and my God." (Psalm 42:5)

*****

As the years passed things settled back into the dysfunctional routine as before. Thus far I had lived my life trying to avoid landmines, trying to fix things, trying to be peacemaker, wife, daughter, mother. Asking God to fix things and then trying to fix them myself. OK, God here it is. Here's the problem. You take it. Oh wait, let me take it back for a minute while I try just one more thing. And after years of praying for peace in my life I came upon words in the book of Isaiah that would change my life forever. "Seek the Lord while he may be found; call on him while he is near. Let the wicked forsake their ways and the unrighteous their thoughts. Let them turn to the Lord, and he will have mercy on them, and to our God, for he will freely pardon."

"For my thoughts are not your thoughts, neither are your ways my ways, declares the Lord. As the heavens are higher than the earth, so are my ways higher than your ways and my thoughts than your thoughts." (Isaiah 55:6-9) I read on and my eyes were opened. Further down I found a promise!

"For you shall go out with joy and be led forth with peace, the mountains and the hills shall break forth before you into singing. And all the trees of the field will clap their hands. Where once there were thorns, fir trees will grow. Instead of briars, myrtle will grow. And this miracle will make the Lord's name very great and be an everlasting sign of God's power and love." (Isaiah 55:12- 13)

I certainly had not been seeking the Lord. I was too busy mulling over challenges in my live, instead of praising God for the victories. He was right beside me all the time, but I seemed to have forgotten that. Suddenly I realized that I had no control over anyone in my life except myself. God was in control even if I didn't understand His thoughts and ways. My situation was a test of my faith. I needed to stop trying to be in charge and start listening to God. The promise jumped off the page at me. God said I will live in peace and joy and all the world around me will rejoice. I had read in my Bible that if we chose not to praise God, the rocks would cry out. (Luke 19:40) Now He reminded me that even the trees would clap their hands!

Finally, He promised that fir trees and myrtle would spring up where once there were thorns. There was hope! I knew unequivocally that God was offering me a promise, if I would claim it. Even the references to natural elements, trees, hills, thorns, myrtle, and firs were a confirmation that God was speaking directly to me.

This was an epiphany! In total despair, I got on my knees and gave my problems, in earnest to the Lord. Why had I not listened to what God was trying to tell me! I placed the situation with my mother and my husband right in God's lap and this time I left it there. Lord, I prayed, I can't do anything more. This is an impossible situation and there is absolutely no way out of it. I cannot change my mother. I cannot change my husband. May Your will be done. I am tired of thorns and briars. I want the fir trees and myrtle you promised. I'm so tired of the heartache.

> I tell you the truth,
> you will weep and mourn while the world rejoices.
> You will grieve, but your grief will turn to joy.
> John 16:20

Chapter 35

Today Mike and I visit a friend who has been in a motorcycle accident. Michael is an elder in our church and one of his spiritual responsibilities is to visit the sick. While our friend is expected to survive, he has a head injury and is still in Upstate Medical Center's Neurosurgical Intensive Care unit. My husband, blessed with the gift of gab, chats quietly with the nurses and holds our friend's hand. I am extremely uncomfortable in here, so much so that I kind of freeze in place. Michael asks if I am OK and I nod stiffly. This place brings back so many memories and makes my heart ache once again.

*****

In early November of 1993, I received a phone call in the middle of the night. I heard my dad's voice, calm and composed, as always, "Jeanne, your mom woke up with, what she called was the worst headache in her life. I took her to the emergency room here in Oneida. They did a cat scan and she is going to Upstate Medical Center in an ambulance. The doctor here told me she had some bleeding in her brain." Immediately my heart began to pound and I tried to shift into nursing mode. Bleeding in her brain I reasoned, could be from an injury (did she fall or hit her head?) It could be a stroke, or even an aneurysm.

"Dad, is she awake? Is she talking? Dad, do you want me to come there and drive you to Upstate?"

"Oh yes, she's awake and talking," my father replied. I did not hear any particular concern in his voice. "No, I can drive myself. I'll follow the ambulance. Can you meet us there?"

"Yes, I'm on my way." I threw on some clothes recklessly and filled Michael in on the scant details. I prayed fervently during the 30-mile drive to the medical center. Dear Lord, this is one of those times when I don't have words to express what's in my heart. I pray that Your will be done. Keep my mom safe and don't take her from us. Bless my father and give me the strength to endure whatever is ahead. Amen.

I found my father in a waiting room. I was full of fear and dread, but tried to cover it up with a confident smile as I hugged my dad. "Your mom is in there," he said, motioning toward a set of double doors. I did not wait for an explanation but went to my mother. She was lying on a stretcher in a small room. Two nurses were moving about quickly, starting IV's, drawing blood, and attaching wires and electrodes to my mother. The nurse informed me that she was being prepped for emergency surgery. I choked down the terror and panic rising in my soul. I followed as the stretcher began to move.

"This is as far as you can go," the nurse said softly.

I smiled down at my mother, kissed her and said, "I love you Mom. I will be right here waiting for you."

"I love you, too." And then, "Are you going to have to shave my head?" I heard my mother ask as they wheeled her toward the operating room.

"Yes, but we do that after you are asleep, Joan. That way you can't protest." I felt better momentarily, knowing my mother was in the hands of capable nurses, with a sense of humor to boot. I returned to my father who had said his goodbyes before I had arrived and now sat, uncomfortable and not knowing quite what to do. A young doctor approached us, huddled there in the waiting room.

He extended his hand toward my father, "Mr. Wilhite? I'm Dr Jones. Your wife needs surgery right away. She has what we call a dissecting cerebral aneurysm. A blood vessel on the left side of her brain has ruptured and there is blood leaking into the brain tissue. The vessel is very close to her optic nerve and it may cause blindness in her left eye. She will have some brain damage from this incident, but I cannot tell you the extent right now. We need to get in there and see if we can fix the vessel with some clips. This surgery is not without considerable risk. Mr. Wilhite, your wife very well may not survive the surgery and if she does, she will not come out of this as the same woman you knew."

My father signed a form giving the neurosurgeon permission to perform the operation. As he handed back the clipboard and pen, my father dropped his head in his hands and wept. Dr. Jones put a sympathetic hand on Dad's shoulder and looked at me.

"The surgery will take at least 8 to 10 hours. I will do my best for her and will be back in touch with you."

I nodded and hugged my father tighter, "Don't cry, Daddy. Please don't cry. It will be OK," I soothed through my own tears. The last time I saw my father cry was the horrible night Mikey was killed and his sobs made me feel like the world was spinning out of control. He collected himself and we prepared to make phone calls to my sister, the grandchildren, friends and Michael. My brother, Jamie was spending a month in Hungary with friends and we decided it was best not to tell him about Mom just yet.

The surgery took close to 10 hours and each hour that ticked by I thanked God that we had not received bad news. Finally, a nurse called us into the hall. Dr. Jones was waiting with his OR cap in his hands.

"Mr. Wilhite, your wife tolerated the surgery pretty well, but there was considerable damage to the cerebral tissue. She is being moved to the neurosurgical intensive care unit now. Any questions?" We were silent, trying to make sense of the cold facts. "She's not out of the woods and has a long road ahead of her," he remarked.

We were allowed, one at a time, to spend 5 minutes in the neurology intensive care unit. Although I was a nurse, I was not prepared for what I witnessed. My mother looked so small and helpless, lying under a canopy of drainage tubes, IV tubing and monitor wires. Her head was completely bandaged and her eyes were shut and swollen. She was as pale as the white sheet that covered her. My heart thumped in my chest as I tried to sort out my thoughts and feelings. I felt alienated from this tiny person lying before me. Was this the person who I feared would wreck my life any day now? Several complicated machines hummed around her bedside. The one thing I did recognize with dismay was the endotracheal tube taped at her mouth. She was on a mechanical ventilator. The machine near the head of the bed was breathing for her. She was completely still except for the rise and fall of her chest as the mechanical ventilator kept her breathing. Oh God, I prayed, not this. As difficult as she has been, I don't want her to die. It was then I remembered His words, "For my thoughts are not your thoughts, neither are your ways my ways."

Within a day, my sister Lynn arrived from her home in Florida. My father and I explained that Mom was in a coma and would not respond. My sister and I hung photos of our families around the bed. The medical staff began allowing us longer visits. Lynn brought in a radio and we played the music that Mom loved, Frank Sinatra and Glenn Miller. She did not wake up.

As the days turned into weeks, I became more comfortable with the medical equipment that was keeping my mother alive. I rubbed her back and lotioned her hands and feet, all the while talking to her and encouraging her. During bath time, I helped her nurses remove the compression leggings that continually massaged her lower extremities to prevent blood clots. I helped to reposition her and swabbed her mouth to moisten dry membranes. God spoke to me often during my time with her and I clearly understood His message. I knew without question that this was why I had become a nurse. You will honor your mother, now and in the days to come.

I was encouraged one day to find the ventilator gone and Mom was breathing unaided. This garnered hope that she would recover. She began moving her arms and reaching for her face. It was then we began to notice a weak grip when we held her hand. Dad was never one to initiate physical touch, but he often held Mom's hand and gently asked her to wake up.

Finally, after almost a month of lying nearly motionless and silent Mom began to awaken. She opened her eyes and seemed to stare at the ceiling. Dad leaned over her to position himself in her line of vision. "Do you think she can see me?" he asked. When he straightened up, she slowly turned her head slightly toward him. Her face was without expression, but she had executed a deliberate action and we rejoiced. We praised her and encouraged her to do more.

The following week she began to try to speak. Her voice was hollow, but we listened for any recognizable word. We pointed to one another and asked, "Mom, do you know who this is?" We were desperate to see a flicker of the old Joanie Wilhite.

"What's my name, Mom? Who am I?" I pressed. We desperately wanted to know that she knew and recognized us.

Finally, the nurse, obviously irritated with us all, announced, "I'm going to have to ask you to leave now. Your mother is exhausted." I looked at Dad and Lynn, embarrassed.

"Well, she's a bossy witch," I said under my breath as we gathered up our things. However, I knew she was right, and I was thankful that she was looking out for her patient's best interest. Shame burned in my heart that I was so selfish and insensitive to my mother's fragile state. I tried, at her expense, to fulfill a deep need to have my mother back.

While she didn't initiate conversation yet, she made us laugh by guessing at answers to our barrage of questions. Her voice had a softness to it and we had to listen closely to her whispers. She insisted that my name was Dr. Fadinski and when Rebecca visited from nearby college, she called her Elizabeth Pee Wee. We all laughed at her bedside and Mom chuckled too, although she didn't really know what was funny. We reminded her who we were over and over and showed her family photos. It was amazing to me that she never asked why she was in the hospital.

One day we arrived to find Mom's head bandages were gone. There, arcing from her left temple up and around her left ear was a huge stapled incision.

Underneath the incision, her skull was uneven, as though someone had taken a hammer and bashed her head, making several concave spots. Her head had been completely shaved for her surgery, but now sprouted hair about 1/8 of an inch long. Near the incision, a drainage tube had been sutured in place and curved under her pillow to a pouch. "Your mom is being transferred upstairs to the neurology unit," her nurse announced happily. Mom smiled brightly, although she had no idea what that meant.

We laughed and celebrated, but once again, Michael was excluded. When Mom began to regain consciousness, Michael thought it best to stop visiting. Surely, his presence would not be conducive to healing after all that had gone on between them. The last thing my mother needed was an emotional upset. I began to visit my mom alone, while Michael waited patiently down the hall.

Finally, we were confident she was going to be all right. Life for the rest of us had to go on. I had taken a leave of absence from my job. Lynn had spent nearly four vigilant weeks with us. She reluctantly returned to Florida after a heartbreaking and uncertain month. I cried uncontrollably for her, my parents and myself when she kissed our mom goodbye.

Mom spent another week in the hospital before being transferred to a rehabilitation center on the other side of the city. It was December already and she had been hospitalized for six weeks.

> Consider it pure joy, my brothers and sisters,
> whenever you face trials of many kinds,
> because you know that the testing of your faith
> produces perseverance.
> James 1:2

Chapter 36

Every day after work Mike and I made the 60-mile round trip to the hospital. It was our time to catch up on each other's lives. Suddenly all the activities with home, church and friends ceased to be a priority for me. We talked about the kids. Becki was a junior at LeMoyne College and Eric was in the Navy, stationed in far away Hawaii.

"The kids haven't called, have they?" I asked. "Michael, I feel like I am out of touch with them both." I turned in my seat to face him. "Thank you for driving me up here," I said, caressing his arm. I had become proficient at creating believable facades during my mother's illness. I was able to appear strong, confident, and optimistic for my family's sake. However, inside I felt like I was crumbling. Michael sacrificed his time to support me during this crisis and he was the only one who knew my personal struggles. Driving to and from the hospital, I could cry and express my fears. Not knowing if my mother would live or die made everything else in my life seem meaningless. I didn't care about the dust bunnies rolling about the house like tumbleweeds or if there was enough milk for breakfast. Our barn animals looked perplexed when we began feeding them at 9:30 pm instead of the usual 5 pm chore time. Our days were long.

Throughout December, we watched and coaxed as Mom improved. She was unable to walk without help, but quickly learned to navigate a wheelchair. She spent her days in physical and occupation therapy sessions. I was included in her care plan meetings and learned how to best help her regain her ability to perform activities of daily living. I met with the physical and occupational therapists, who helped me gain direction and the determination to help my mother. I was cognizant of just how far we had to go.

I sat across the table from her and placed a ball, a ring of keys, and a small book in front of her. "Mom, can you pick up the ball please?" I would ask, smiling at her. She looked confused, picked up the keys, and handed them to me, as if to say, is this what you want?

"Nope, try again, Mom," I corrected. I patted her hand, "It's OK, you'll get it." As I lined up the objects again, I repeated, "This is a ball. This is a book. These are keys." At times, it was discouraging that she had so much difficulty mentally processing the spoken word. Will she ever be able to read again? I wondered. Slowly her mental capacity improved.

We all marveled at the funny things she said. She finally stopped calling me Dr. Fadinski. The first time I heard her say my name reminded me of the first time our kids said 'Mama.' It was a sweet sound. I knew my mom was coming back. She was able to articulate better and better each day. She began to recognize when she used a word wrong, even if she couldn't call up the right word.

Dad and I celebrated Christmas at the rehab center and it broke my heart that Mom had no idea what the holiday was about. She opened her gifts mechanically when we told her to. The little Christmas tree, decorations, and goodies were my attempt to make a special celebration for the person who always made Christmas magical and bigger than life for me. That Christmas Mom received two turbans and a funny plaid golf hat to keep her bare head warm, a radio that played music cassettes and a white board to practice letters on.

I walked into her room one day and found her restrained in her wheelchair, her face bruised, and ugly black stitches tracking along her left eyebrow. She reached her hand out to me as though she had done something wrong. "Hi Joanie," I said, giving her a hug, "I'll be right back, Mom." I went to the desk and demanded to know what had happened.

"She fell out of bed last night." was the cold, simple response. Apparently this must have been a common occurrence, for the nurse showed no concern or compassion at all. I was angry. Didn't they know that this was my mother? Her care and safety were entrusted to them. I felt betrayed. Obviously, no one there could care for my mother in the way I wanted while she was in this vulnerable, childlike state. I spent the rest of the time my mom was in the rehab center like an overprotective mother bear. She was my cub and I would challenge anything or anybody who jeopardized her well-being. I loved her more and more each day.

We were playing a matching game when my mother looked up and asked, "Jeanne, where is Michael?" I didn't know if she was asking about her deceased son or my husband. I held my breath and quickly decided that this was not the time to remind her of her son's death.

"You mean my Michael, Mom?"

She nodded and continued, "Why hasn't he come here to see me?" I exhaled but forgot to breathe again. She looked at me, perplexed and searched my face for an answer.

"Mom, Michael hasn't visited because he hasn't wanted to upset you. Don't you remember? You two have been at odds with each other for years."

She shook her nearly bald head vigorously, "No, No, I want to see him! Will you bring him to visit next time?"

"OK, Mom, sure I will," was all I could stammer.

God bless Michael. He agreed to accompany me on my next trip to the rehabilitation center. When we arrived, Mom sat in her wheelchair, rocking it back and forth quietly as she stared out the window. She was wearing the funny plaid hat we had given her at Christmas.

"So how are you doin'?" he said gently, as we entered her room. She turned the wheelchair around and squeezed her left eye shut, to correct the double vision she had experienced since the aneurysm. She smiled and began wiggling her fingers in front of her face. She had acquired this new gesture since her aneurysm, especially when she was preparing to speak.

"I know you!" she said to Mike.

"Yea? Do you remember my name?" Michael asked.

"Well of course I do!" She reached for his hand and held it, her own hands trembling. "Your name is.......umm.

Jeanne, what's his name?" she said as though she was simply flustered from a brief and temporary memory loss.

"Michael. His name is Michael, Mom."

She smiled and patted his hand, "Yes, Michael." Then Mom embraced him like she hadn't seen him in a lifetime. In a way, I guess she hadn't. They chatted effortlessly and I could see that Mike was discovering the limitations and changes that the aneurysm had caused.

Eventually she went home again and while the brain injury was apparent, she did remarkably well.

> Finally, all of you, live in harmony with one another, be sympathetic, love one another, be compassionate and humble. Do not repay evil with evil or insult with insult, but with blessing, because to this you were called so that you may inherit a blessing.
> 1 Peter 3:8-9

Chapter 37

Mom returned home on Valentine's Day in 1994. Her return brought new challenges for us all, but especially Dad. I spent most of my free time there during the first weeks. I sorted out countless medications and put labels on the containers so Dad would know what to give and when. Michael and I moved furniture out of the way to accommodate a walker and commode. I went to the market and bought groceries, including easy-to-swallow soft foods for Mom and juices that she liked. I grabbed a big container of mixed nuts for Dad and bought foods that would be easy for him to prepare in my absence.

I watched as my frustrated father sat at the big mahogany desk in the living room and tried to sort through the mounting pile of hospital bills and notices from the insurance company. He turned to ask Mom a question about the checkbook. Then, knowing she was unable to give him an answer, he threw his pen aside. He wandered into the kitchen to fix himself another cup of coffee, his answer to most of life's problems. Mom had always taken care of the finances for their household, but now she sat in adult diapers, tapping her fingers aimlessly on the TV table we had set up beside her chair in the living room.

Each evening before I left I made sure Mom was washed up, in clean pajamas and tucked into bed. I sat on the edge of the bed and gently stroked Mom's fuzzy head. My fingers rippled over the fresh scar and uneven contours of her skull. It brought to mind how much I loved it when she caressed my hair and called me "Babe" when I was sick as a child. Roles were changing. I embraced the notion and I knew that with God's help and divine leading, I was up to the challenge of whatever lay ahead. Through tears, I prayed for my mother as her eyes fluttered and then closed in mindless slumber. I thanked God for giving me the opportunity to make up for the years when I was rebellious.

We put pillows from the guest rooms upstairs on the floor along side the bed, in case she rolled out of bed. I cautioned my father not to trip over the 'soft landing' on Mom's side of the bed. I felt good knowing Dad would have a few minutes to relax before he turned in for the night exhausted. Reminding them that I would return early the next morning, I left my parents, reunited again after three and a half long uncertain months.

On the fourth day home, Mom seemed more lethargic and my mindset switched from daughter to nurse. When she did not attempt to feed herself breakfast, I began spooning oatmeal into her mouth. She held the cereal in her mouth and stared at me with drowsy eyes. "Swallow, Mom," I coaxed. Finally, I removed the food from her mouth with my fingers as she began to snore. I dialed Dr. Jones's office and explained how listless and sleepy my mom had become. I knew something was wrong. The nurse tried to minimize the situation and implied I was overreacting. But I was insistent that she be seen immediately. I knew a significant change in one's level of consciousness was a red flag in neurologic post-operative patients.

We bundled her up and returned to Syracuse. We quickly learned that Mom's intracranial pressure was elevated and she was hospitalized again for placement of a shunt. The VP shunt or Ventricular-Peritoneal Shunt drained extra fluid from her brain into her abdominal cavity where it was absorbed. She was back home within a few days, much more alert.

Mom was strong in spirit and in body and she improved week by week. Her eyeglasses were fitted with a black lens on the left to help with double vision issues. She would wear what we called, the 'Pirate's Patch' for the rest of her life. But she no longer needed to close her left eye to avoid double vision. She learned to walk without the aid of a walker. Her physical strength returned, as did her ability to reason, and communicate effectively.

I began taking Mom out to lunch once or twice a week, not only to spend time with her, but to give Dad a break from the constant attention she needed. Jamie, now 30 years old, was single and spent much of his time trying to help Dad as well. It was a lesson in patience for me each time I helped her navigate down the front steps and into my car. She took one slow step at a time and paused in between as if concentrating on how to execute the next movement. We talked and I gently corrected when she used a word wrong and offered words when none would come to her. "How is your little...." and she began to waggle her fingers and look at a me with desperation.

I held her trembling hand and asked, "Cat? How is my little cat, Mom?"

"No." Her hand continued to shake under mine.

"Dog?"

"Yes!" she answered triumphantly, "How is your little dog?" Dottie, our beloved Boston Terrier and successor to Emily, was Mom's new favorite.

I saw improvement every week. The old Mom's spunky personality returned, but gone were her controlling ways. She needed me and I was able to be there for her, as a daughter and as a nurse. For the first time in my life, I felt like I was honoring my mother.

When we went out, I taught her how to order from a menu and how to count money and pay for a meal. I became proficient at knowing what she wanted to say before she even attempted to speak. Her endearing gesture when she was unable to articulate reminded me of a magician attempting to conjure up some hocus-pocus. She brought her right hand up and wiggled her fingers in front of her lips, as if trying to magically articulate. After our lunch dates, I often brought Mom to our house. She would sit at the dining room table where we'd fold laundry together or practice using the telephone. We reviewed simple recipes, discussed what they meant and then I'd help her cook or bake. It was rewarding for her and me when she successfully baked cookies for Dad under my watchful eye.

I told her jokes and then explained why they were funny. Sometimes we played simple games or looked at magazines and discussed what we saw on the pages. I asked leading questions to encourage her to verbalize her thoughts. She eventually learned to read again and her speech improved significantly. It was a joy to be around her. She was childlike at times, but I saw her old personality emerging.

God had worked a divine miracle of sorts and completely transformed the part of my mother's brain that was responsible for her disruptive nature. She loved Michael and would often tell him so. Gone were the critical spirit, the manipulation and the mind games. Never again were there cross words between her and Mike. She was pure, non-judgmental and sweet.

Often she struggled with the simplest task and I wondered why God allowed the aneurysm to occur. Could it be to stop the ongoing battle between her and my husband? It sounded crazy, but I knew God worked in mysterious ways and in His time, not ours.

Dad reluctantly took over the responsibility of running the household on Stroud Street for the next five years. Peace reigned on all fronts. They settled into a comfortable routine and I felt my parents, now headed into their 70's, were safe. Although Lynn lived away, Jamie, spent lots of time with them.

Michael and I adjusted to life alone. Our kids were now grown and safely on their own. Rebecca had a beautiful wedding, and when I was 45 years old, it was my turn to live vicariously through my daughter. Helping with the wedding plans and experiencing the ceremony and reception gave me the chance to finally come to terms with my long-standing grief over all I had missed on my wedding day.

Eric was married, lived in California and blessed us with our first grandchild, Chelsea, born in 1992. Becki and her husband, Eric (yes, our son and son-in-law have the same first name) gave us granddaughter, Tabitha in 1998. Nicholas, our son's second baby, came soon after Tabitha. God had blessed us with three beautiful grandchildren. Because both of our kids had made decisions for Christ, we rested in the assurance that our grandchildren, too, would be raised to know and love Jesus.

Michael and I discovered the pleasure of traveling. We explored far-flung places like Russia and Argentina. We walked on the Great Wall of China, kissed the Blarney Stone in Ireland and swam with sharks on the Great Barrier Reef. My life was so full and rewarding. We grew in service to the Lord and His blessings flowed freely into our lives. We obeyed Jesus' great commission to go into all the world to spread the good news. We traveled several times to New York City to minister to the homeless there. We were privileged to share the gospel on several short-term mission trips, including a week in Cuba.

On our homestead, we were always busy. We built an authentic log cabin in our woods, with the help of our team of Percheron draft horses, Ben and Bill. It was built entirely of hemlock logs from our own woods and our family used it as a retreat. We became licensed wildlife rehabilitators and took in injured and orphaned wild animals. We enjoyed watching our grandchildren grow and I became known as, "Onnie," the name my grandchildren would call me for the rest of my life. We sang and played guitars with the worship team at church and facilitated a long-standing Bible study on marriage. God's hand was upon us.

Then my beloved father was diagnosed with an aggressive form of bladder cancer. I rallied around him when he had radical ileostomy surgery and struggled with the change in his body image. I put my nursing skills and knowledge to work once again. As a nurse, changing an ileostomy dressing or bag was routine for me. I made light of the whole matter and assured him that he was still my favorite dad. Lynn came from Florida again and together we tried to ease our sorrow as we watched our dad grow weaker. Eleven months after his diagnosis, with dignity and courage, he lost his battle and passed away.

Mom's strength during this difficult time amazed me. Despite her residual limitations from her aneurysm, she was strong in mind, body and spirit. She displayed incredible faith in God that I never knew she possessed. But now she was alone in the lovely four bedroom Cape Cod house on Stroud Street and she did not want to leave. She did not want to lose the autonomy she had worked so hard to regain.

We made Mom promise not to go upstairs or into the basement. Michael spent several days moving the washer and dryer up from the basement, along with all the venting and electrical wiring. She could live comfortably on the main floor. Now, once again, we fretted and worried about her safety. Jamie more or less moved back in with her and, although he had his own unease and turmoil to deal with, we were thankful someone was there with her.

Jeanne Wilhite Dunn

> Better a patient person than a warrior,
> one who controls his temper,
> than one who takes a city.
> Proverbs 16:32

Chapter 38

My bilateral knee replacements preclude me from getting down on my knees. It is nearly impossible for me to crawl around in the attic, so I enlist some help. "Hey, girls, want to earn some spending money?" I ask our granddaughters, Tabitha and Kylie, who are spending the weekend with us from their home in Rochester. At 17 and 14, respectively, they scramble into the attic like two little mice and help me to organize and label hidden treasures.

"Hey, here's the cane you used when you had your knees fixed! The one you painted the ladybugs on."

"Onnie, I found a box of old photos of Gram and Pop Wilhite!" The girls' voices are muffled in the confines of narrow spaces between boxes and bags. I sit in the doorway to the attic and think about the unbearable pain I had experienced before my knee surgeries. My mother encountered the same agony and passed her

arthritic knees down to me. I can't help but recall with sorrow the catastrophe of my mother's knee replacement surgery.

*****

The day had been perfect. The sun shone brightly and the zinnias and cosmos teased the bees by swaying this way and that in the gentle breeze. In the summer, my dryer didn't get much use because I chose to hang the freshly laundered sheets and towels on the clothesline behind the garage. It was late in the afternoon. I finished my glass of lemonade on the porch swing and sauntered out past the garage to bring the wash in. Just as I folded the first towel and placed it in the wicker clothesbasket, Mike arrived with my mother in the car. He had volunteered to take Mom to a doctor's appointment earlier in the afternoon. As he helped my mother out of the car he called, "Did you know she had an appointment with an orthopedic surgeon today?"

Surprised, I turned to face him. "No. What are you talking about? I thought she was going for a checkup." I stopped dropping clothespins in the basket and left a towel hanging precariously by one corner.

Mom hobbled out to the clothesline where I stood in disbelief. "I'm going to have a knee replacement in 2 weeks," she announced.

"Mom!" I shouted a little too loudly, "We have talked about this before! Lynn and I tried to get you to have the surgery before your aneurysm and you refused to do it. Now you're not a good candidate for an operation like that!" I yanked clothespins off the line and threw the linens into the oval wicker basket. "Get in the car and I'll take you home." I said angrily. "I knew nothing about this."

Although he was not at fault, I glared at Michael and stomped off to the car. He shrugged his shoulders. "I just took her where she told me to go." Dad had been gone a year already and I had become accustomed to being the person in command of my mother. Not only was I her power of attorney, but I was involved with every aspect of her life.

I got in the car and slammed the door on the sunny day. I turned in my seat to face my mother, who sat like a little girl waiting for her punishment. Her pitiful countenance did not soften my heart. "Mom, please don't talk to me right now. I am so angry with you, I am apt to say something I'll regret." She was silent and turned toward the passenger window, pretending to inspect the flowers that bloomed along the porch. Or maybe her attention was on the periwinkle flowers that bloomed on the myrtle growing there. In any case, I knew she was trying to avoid my wrath.

I backed the car out of the driveway and headed toward Canastota. The air in the car was thick with my anger and frustration over, what I perceived as, her rash decision. "Why in the world would you decide to have a knee replacement now? You should have done it when you were healthier. We tried to get you to have the surgery long ago, but you were too stubborn to do it. Don't you realize the circulation in your brain has been compromised?" She did not respond so I continued to blast her. "Do you know you could develop a blood clot from joint replacement surgery? It could travel to your heart or lungs or brain." I stopped the car in front of her house and she nodded and looked toward the front door. "And do you realize that means you could have a heart attack or a stroke? One that might even kill you?" I paused. Why was I so outraged? I tried to decide if it was because she had usurped my role as caretaker or because she would dare to put me through more anguish by endangering her own life. Either way, I was reacting selfishly to a choice that was hers to make.

As I tried to collect my thoughts, she looked me squarely in the eye and replied, "Well, your Daddy is gone and I don't care if I do die." She opened the car door, struggled to get out, and quietly closed the door. I watched as she made her way slowly and painfully up the front steps. Her rocking gait ceased and she fumbled to open the front door. She turned before entering the house and waved goodbye.

I waved back, drove a block away and burst into tears. I was ashamed that I had mistreated my own mother. My callous words had spilled out of my mouth like poison. She certainly didn't deserve such treatment, especially when she had experienced unrelenting pain in her knees for such a long time. I prayed for forgiveness and promised God I would support my mom without wavering in her choosing to go ahead with this risky surgery. I dried my tears, put the car in gear and headed home. I will walk through this with her, I said to God, but I do not have a good feeling about it.

Mom had her knee replacement and both Mike and I were there from start to finish. We visited her often for the few days she was hospitalized. We arranged for her to go to the extended care facility that was affiliated with the hospital where I worked. She would receive physical therapy there until she was ready to return home with her new knee. Everything seemed to have gone off without a hitch. When we visited her the night before discharge from the hospital, she reminded us to bring her slippers so she could walk to the car when discharged. She was optimistic and enthusiastic.

Rebecca was home from college so she and I arrived at the hospital on discharge day. As soon as we walked into her room, I knew something was terribly wrong. Mom was lethargic, her speech was slurred, and her left arm was limp. I knew my worst fear had become a reality. Mom had suffered a cerebral vascular accident, or stroke, as a result of her knee surgery. Dear Jesus, I prayed, fill me with Your peace that surpasses all understanding. I am so fearful that this may be the beginning of the end.

Rebecca and I got Mom safely to the extended care facility. Tests indicated that she had, indeed, suffered a stroke. Physical therapy was a complicated challenge now. Her speech improved some, but the independence for which she had worked so hard was gone. She needed 24-hour nursing care. The stroke affected her ability to swallow and all treatment modalities failed. Although she received intravenous fluids, she was starving to death. I explained that a simple surgery was available to put a tube into her stomach through the abdominal wall so she could get liquid nourishment. "Do you want to go ahead and have the tube placed, Mom?" I asked, "Otherwise you are not able to get enough nourishment to sustain life." I knew I owed her the plain truth in words she was able to understand. This was her choice to make and this time I would not dishonor her by questioning her decision.

And her decision was an emphatic, "No." To be sure she understood, I repeated the options. While I did, she shook her head insistently and repeated, "No, no, no. I don't want it."

As the weeks dragged on, my mother grew weaker and weaker. God in His mercy provided both Michael and me a precious opportunity to spend meaningful time with her. Michael was kind enough to take her to doctor appointments and for an occasional drive to get her out of the nursing home. Because she could no longer walk, he would lift my mother in and out of her wheelchair in his arms. Only God could have arranged this circumstance and it brought tears to my eyes to watch their tender interactions.

Jeanne Wilhite Dunn

> But seek first his kingdom and his righteousness,
> and all these things will be given to you as well.
> Matthew 6:33

Chapter 39

Kylie, our fourth and youngest grandchild is going to be 14 years old this Thanksgiving. "Kylie, we hate to miss your birthday. Are you sure you can celebrate without us?" Michael teases. She tosses her long blonde hair and giggles.

"Oh, I don't know, Poppa. I'll try." The cell phone in Kylie's hand chirps out a funny sound and she turns back to text or Snapchat or whatever it is she does with that thing. All of our grandkids are technology wizards, which makes Michael and me realize we are now officially considered old-fashioned. We are excited to be going to Tennessee to spend the holiday with Eric, his wife Lori, and their blended family. They even invited our two Boston Terriers, Kitzel and Greta to come along.

Kylie is our sensitive one. Her gift is her compassion and desire to help others. Unfortunately she holds the distinction of being the only great-grandchild in our family that my mother never got to hold. I think back to the extraordinary circumstances on the day Kylie was born.

*****

Three months after she suffered the stroke, Mom passed away at the age of 72. It had been a year since my father's death. As a nurse, I could see several weeks in advance that my mom was slipping away. Her death was eminent, we had called Lynn to come and now sent Jamie to the airport to pick her up.

Michael and I sat at my mother's bedside in the nursing home with heavy hearts. I gazed at her quiet face. Images fluttered through my mind like an old slide show running in reverse, as I recalled many memories, both sorrowful and joyous. I thought of how her grandchildren especially, had brought Mom so much joy. As adults, they loved to tease Gram and she affectionately teased right back. When her great grandchildren started to arrive, Mom was content to simply rock them as she gazed happily at their tiny faces. She drew tremendous satisfaction and pride in her family as it grew.

I thought of Rebecca. I was riding an emotional pendulum with a dying mother and a daughter whose baby was due any minute. I had difficulty directing my thoughts and attention between them.

We waited eagerly for the arrival of our fourth and final grandchild. I had called Becki earlier in the day. "Hi Becki, how are you doing?" I asked, "Any contractions yet?" The date the baby was due had come and gone.

"No Mom, nothing yet. I wish I could be there with Gram and you and Dad. How are you guys doing?"

"We are OK, Becki. Jamie just left to pick up Lynn at the airport in Syracuse. I hope they make it back before Gram is gone."

Becki's voice was choked with tears, "Tell Grammy I love her, Mom."

"I will. We love you Beck. Take care. We'll call you later." I hung up the phone and dabbed at my eyes.

We both knew Gram would never see this little one yet unborn. We said goodbye in tears and I returned to Mom's bedside. I felt the familiar misery of being torn between two loved ones. Rebecca wanted so badly for both her dad and me to be there when she went into labor, but I knew I needed to be at my mother's side during her last hours. With Becki and her husband Eric living two hours away in Rochester, NY, I simply put the situation in God's hands and prayed that He would work things out. Heavenly Father, I prayed, please make this easy for my mother. I love her so much. I stroked her dry, withered hand and whispered words of love and encouragement to her. Later that same evening, Jamie and Lynn arrived and we all had the opportunity to say our final goodbyes. As I held my mom's hand, she slipped away into eternity.

But according to God's Word, joy comes in the morning. and our joy was on its way! "For his anger lasts only a moment, but his favor lasts a lifetime; weeping may stay for the night, but rejoicing comes in the morning." (Psalm 30:5)

Michael and I returned home, made the necessary phone calls to family and settled into bed with grieving hearts. A few hours later the phone startled us and Rebecca's voice rang sweet in our ears, "Mom, Dad, the baby's coming! Eric is taking me to the hospital in a few minutes. Meet us there, OK?"

"We're on our way!" Mike said excitedly. We showered, dressed and started out on the long trip to Rochester, praying all along the way that we would make it before the baby was born. When we arrived at the hospital we found our way to the OB unit. A nurse sat at the desk in scrubs printed with pink and blue booties. She looked up and smiled.

"We are looking for Rebecca Truelson. She's our daughter." The nurse widened her smile and pointed down the corridor. Eric and Rebecca walked toward us, dragging an IV pole, a badge of initiation into the world of obstetrics.

"The nurses said if I walk my labor will progress faster," she said, smiling as she rubbed her rotund tummy. Rebecca is blessed with my mother's endless energy and, like my Mom, she is totally dedicated to her family.

She reached out and gave me a long hug, "I'm so sorry Mom." We cried together for the loss of the family matriarch we loved. Becki would have given anything to be with Gram and me during my mother's last days, but she was unable to travel so late in her pregnancy. She called often and was a wonderful support to me, as she always is.

Becki's labor progressed through the night and I thanked God for the forthcoming gift of a child and His faithfulness to me. I asked for God's mercy as I held Rebecca's hand through each contraction. As I stroked her smooth skin, I thought of my mother and how I had held her hand just hours before. Heavenly Father, I prayed, please make this easy for my daughter. I love her so much.

Suddenly Kylie Shay Truelson, our newest granddaughter arrived and took her first breath. Her beautiful cry filled the room with hope, with life, and with elation. At that very moment both grief and joy flooded my soul. Witnessing the death of my mother and the birth of my granddaughter, I could only celebrate God's wonderful miracle and plan for our days here on earth. I believe Kylie was born at a time ordained by God, as a sign of hope and renewal in my life. She, along with our other grandchildren became the fir trees that God had promised and an everlasting sign of God's power and love.

> Be still and know that I am God.
> Psalm 46:10

Epilogue

Another October is upon us and my life continues to be as rich and colorful as the leaves that drift down to earth. I put away the bird bath and mulch the roses for the last time before winter. I am thankful for the gift of each new day and try to live it to bring glory to God.

Michael often tells Eric and Rebecca that we have exchanged our youth for wisdom. I'm not sure if its wisdom as much as courage. It takes courage to be a parent. I remember with amazing clarity the struggles my mother and I had, the calamity of her illness and the lessons God taught me through all of it. As Ben Franklin said, "Those things that hurt, instruct." The wounds from the thorns during that time in my life have healed, and I have discovered that on the other side of pain lies strength.

I was not a perfect mother when it was my turn, but I was able to trust in the strength of the Lord when strife camped on my doorstep. I rejoice in my heart knowing that throughout my life I have received miraculous answers to impossible prayers. God's perfect plan is sovereign. Never underestimate the power of the Living God!

Michael joins me in the yard. His silver-white hair glints in the autumn sunshine as he moves toward me. "You, my love, are so handsome," I say. I take his weathered face in my hands and kiss him square on the mouth. My love for him still overflows even after 46 years of marriage.

Slowly, hand in hand, we make our way out back to a stand of evergreens beside the pond. Our fir trees grow there, brushing the fall clouds along their way in the cerulean sky. I remember God's promise and I delight in the assurance that the firs will stay ever green, even through the winter of our lives. Michael parts the fragrant boughs for me to reveal an empty nest there in the branches. There is no need to speak. We smile at each other, knowing the other's heart.

The End

My mother, Joan Helene, between her parents, a few years before they divorced. Her father was Albert Peter Wechner(Pagar) and her mother was Elsie Wagner Wechner.(Nana)
1930

The Wilhites in 1958
Me (age 8) Mom, Lynn (age 12) & Dad

Michael and me the night
of our Senior Ball 1968

Michael and I pose on the hood of his car in front of my Brockport dorm in the fall of 1968

My brothers, Jamie and Mikey, six months before Mikey was killed in 1984

*The painful years visiting my parents
without Michael*

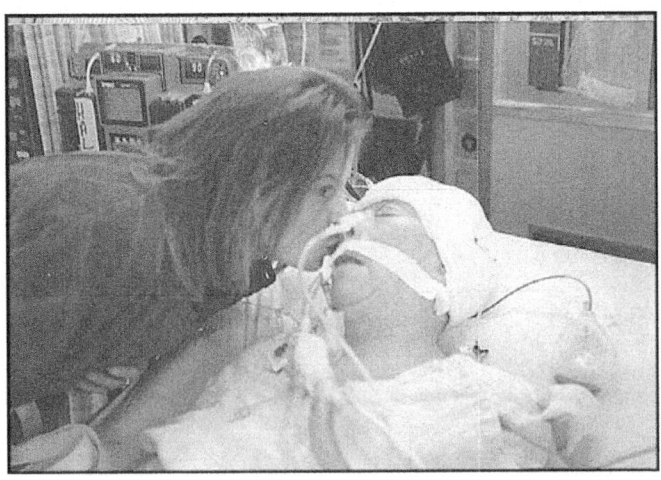

*Rebecca kisses her comatose 'Gram'
after her aneurysm surgery.*

*Mom works hard at the rehab center.
Here we share a laugh over something silly*

*I help Rebecca as she dresses in her
beautiful wedding gown in November 1994.*

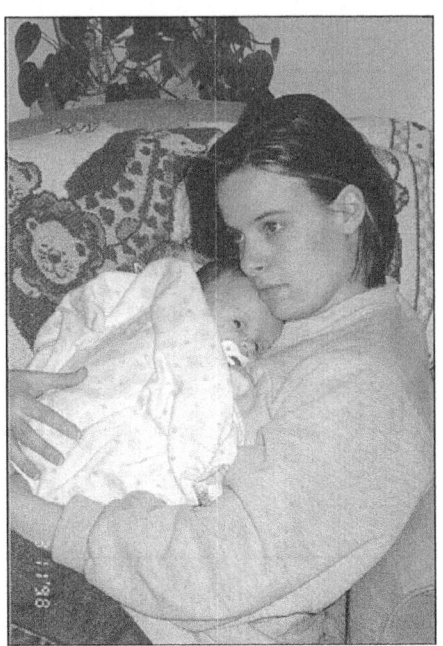

Rebecca and our granddaughter, Kylie, born 18 hours after my mother's death in 2000.

Our adult kids, Becki, Eric & I surround Michael on his 64th birthday.

Our grandchildren in 2004
Nicholas, Kylie, Chelsea & Tabitha.

Eric's family in 2014
Carly, Chelsea, Lori, Eric, Gabriel & Nicholas.

Rebecca's family in 2014
Rebecca, Tabitha, Kylie, & Eric

Michael stands in front of our home on
Frog Hollow Homestead.

Michael and me in 2015
Love never fails.

Made in the USA
Columbia, SC
15 April 2021